SERVING SENIORS

A How-To-Do-It Manual for Librarians

RoseMary Honnold
Saralyn A. Mesaros

**HOW-TO-DO-IT MANUALS
FOR LIBRARIANS**

NUMBER 127

NEAL–SCHUMAN PUBLISHERS, INC.
New York, London

Be sure to visit
http://www.cplrmh.com/seniors.html

The companion Web site that accompanies this book offers hyperlinked resources to save you the time and trouble of typing in long URLs.

It will also keep these resources updated.

Published by Neal-Schuman Publishers, Inc.
100 William Street, Suite 2004
New York, NY 10038

The paper used in this publication meets the minimum requirements of American National Standard for Informational Sciences—Permanence of Paper for Printed Library Materials, ANSI Z39.48—1992

Printed and bound in the United States of America.

Library of Congress Cataloging-in-Publication Data

Honnold, RoseMary, 1954–
    Serving seniors: a how-to-do-it manual for librarians / RoseMary Honnold, Saralyn A. Mesaros.
    p. cm. – (How-to-do-it manual for librarians ; no. 127)
    Includes bibliographical references and index.
    ISBN 1-55570-482-4 (alk. paper)
    1. Libraries and the aged. I. Mesaros, Saralyn A., 1951-II. Title. III. How-to-do-it manual for librarians ; no. 127.

Z711.92.A35H66 2004
027.622-dc21

2003059945

TABLE OF CONTENTS

LIST OF FIGURES

PREFACE

We designed *Serving Seniors: A How-To-Do-It Manual for Librarians* as a hands-on guide for libraries with budgets of all sizes that want wide-ranging, practical, and field-tested ideas to begin or expand services to the older adults in their communities. We address the specific needs of this important group of patrons, including planning, collection development, discussion groups, program ideas, partnering options, and outreach services in the community.

Most libraries try to maintain active, vibrant Children's or Young Adult Departments; *Serving Seniors* advocates building or expanding a lively Senior Services Department. We recommend strategies and programs that reject the cliché "illness model" (still all-too-prevalent in library planning) and instead promote staying well, active, and healthy.

The only word that accurately describes today's senior audience is *diverse*. Chronological age is just one factor to consider. Experience, cultural background, gender, race, expectations, outlook, general health, and financial situation are but a few of the many variables influencing seniors' needs for information and entertainment. As the Baby Boomer generation quickly approaches retirement, innovative and expanded library services for seniors will become even more important in the next few decades.

Part I, "How to Bring Seniors into the Library," tells of the many services you can provide for those who can travel to the library. Learning key information about your elderly patrons will help you agree on the best services and materials your library might provide. Chapter 1, "Develop a Comprehensive Senior Plan," first explores the larger picture of this age group in our country. Then it offers a five-step plan to help you define your area's specific audience, find out who they are, determine where they live, and assess what they need. It helps you consider different ways to successfully meet those needs and communicate their availability to the community.

Chapter 2, "Build a Collection for Senior Adults," delivers tips on building a collection for the senior audience, including formats and equipment helpful to seniors and vendors where you can purchase the items.

Chapter 3, "Start a Discussion Group," investigates the many possibilities beyond the long-time library institution of the book discussion. How about film discussion groups that tie in to books? We recommend a years worth of "Coffee Club" discussion topics—from poetry to gardening to frugal living—all promoting the library's collection.

Chapter 4, "Offer Informative and Entertaining Programs at the Library," shares the many creative and inspiring program ideas from the libraries that contributed to *Serving Seniors*. They range from cooking to crafts, history to hobbies, and travel to writing memoirs. The chapter includes descriptions and instructions for programs you can do yourself, as well as programs that feature speakers from the community.

Chapter 5, "Partner with Outside Agencies," showcases several winning programs. We discuss the benefits of libraries connecting with other organizations, and to get you thinking of the possibilities in your community, we include a list of suggested allies.

Chapter 6, "Mix Seniors with Teens and Children," spotlights intergenerational programs. This chapter presents interesting computer and oral history programs mixing seniors and teens and also illustrates six ready-to-go "Grandparents Day" programs.

Chapter 7, "Surf the Net with Seniors," guides you through the best ways to introduce computers through classes both in the library and off-site. It supplies valuable tips on what material to cover and how to present it, information on assistive technology, and an annotated list of Web sites senior citizens will enjoy and understand.

Chapter 8, "Groom Great Volunteers," offers suggestions for training volunteers, jobs to tackle, and the basics of starting a Friends of the Library group to assure you will have great volunteers at your library.

Part II, "How to Deliver Services to Seniors Where they Live," gives ideas for services and programs for those who are unable to come to the library. Chapter 9, "Take the Library to the Homebound," tells how to start a homebound service through Books-By-Mail or personal delivery by library staff or volunteers.

Chapter 10, "Take the Library to Residential Facilities," shows how to establish book deposit collections and lobby stops at senior residences, nursing homes, and adult day care centers.

Chapter 11, "Take Your Programs to Residential Facilities," lists many programs you can do at these same facilities. We propose programming for times you want to inspire memories, celebrate seasons and holidays, or just offer fun activities that will bring the library to the seniors. All are easy and inexpensive to prepare.

A section of "Additional Resources" for serving seniors completes the book.

- Appendix A is the blank questionnaire we sent to all the libraries that replied to our postings on discussion lists and inquiring e-mails about their own senior lineup. We owe a great deal of thanks to these fellow librarians for their willingness to share their successes so more seniors may benefit from their programs and service ideas.

- Appendix B lists all of those wonderful professionals and the libraries that support their efforts. Visit their Web sites to keep up with their future ideas.

- Appendix C collects the advice and wisdom from our questionnaire respondents. Their sharing of real-life experiences with what works best gives you a head start in developing a great program.

- Appendix D is a list of electronic resources you will find useful, including ALA and CLA sites, electronic discussion lists, and Web sites many public libraries have developed just for seniors.

- Appendix E is a collection of booklists useful for programming and collection development.

- Appendix F is a list of recommended ESL resources for seniors shared by librarians working in multicultural communities.

We, the authors, work at Ohio's Coshocton Public Library. In 1989, RoseMary Honnold began our senior services with a homebound service that started as an extension of the bookmobile department. Book deposits to nursing homes were soon added and, in 1996, Saralyn Mesaros was hired as an Outreach Coordinator to oversee those services. She soon added programming for the nursing homes and assisted living facilities. More programs of interest to senior adults have been presented in the library, and Saralyn's title has evolved to Senior Services Coordinator.

Our senior audience has shown appreciation for these services in many ways. Many make memorial contributions for books and other materials, include the library as a beneficiary; some send cards and gifts of baked goods and candy at holiday times; all share smiles and hugs and say many thank yous.

Two of our oldest patrons are a complete joy and inspiration to all the library staff. Hazel, at 103 years old, still visits the library when her neighbor brings her and is served by the Senior Services Department between visits. She reads nonstop, and her interests include the Civil War and historical romance. She remembers all of our names and always has a smile and an ornery joke to tell. Fern is a 96-year-old homebound patron who listens to an average of eight to twelve audio books every two weeks. Her reading interests are history and biographies, and she loves to visit and hear news of the people and the events in the community. Both of these ladies take things as they come, remain interested and connected, still enjoy the library and the joy of reading, and give us important lessons on growing older gracefully. *Serving Seniors* is fun and rewarding for the seniors and inspiring for the librarians lucky enough to serve them.

ACKNOWLEDGMENTS

Thank you:

To Charles Harmon, the director of publishing at Neal-Schuman, for the opportunity to write this book.

A special thank you to our editor, Michael Kelley, for his never-ending patience, encouragement, and humor with these new authors.

To Ann Miller, the director of Coshocton Public Library, for supporting our programming ideas.

To the many libraries listed in Appendix B for generously sharing their experiences and ideas so this book could be useful for libraries of all sizes in all settings.

To our husbands and families for their support, encouragement, and willingness to overlook what doesn't get done while we write!

PART I: HOW TO BRING SENIORS INTO THE LIBRARY

1 DEVELOP A COMPREHENSIVE SENIOR SERVICES PLAN

The road leading to a goal does not separate you from the destination; it is essentially a part of it.

—Charles DeLint

Have you read your library's mission statement? The goal of a library mission statement is to provide information, entertainment, intellectual development, and enrichment to all the residents of a community regardless of race, creed, politics, or age. Programs for children from birth to the teen years, offered by special library departments and librarians, keep parents and their families coming back to the library for these materials and programs. Bestsellers, home improvement information, videos, childrearing books, cookery collections, technology information, job seeking aids, and many other collections are kept up to date and ready to meet the needs of these busy growing families.

BE AWARE THAT AMERICA IS GETTING OLDER

One of the fastest growing populations in the country is the over-fifty crowd. Take a look at these statistics:

- According to the "New Profile of Senior Citizens" published by the Administration on Aging, as of February 2002 about one out of every eight Americans is now sixty-five years of age or older.
- Since 1900, the percentage of Americans sixty-five and older has more than tripled (4.1 percent in 1900 to 12.4 percent in 2000), and the number has increased from 3.1 million to 35 million.
- By 2030, there will be about seventy million older persons, more than twice their number in 2000.
- In 2000, the sixty-five to seventy-four age group (18.4 million) was eight times larger than in 1900,

but the seventy-five to eighty-four group (12.4 million) was sixteen times larger and the eighty-five and older group (4.2 million) was thirty-four times larger!

- According to Aging in America, the eighty-five and older group is currently the fastest growing segment in the population.

TODAY'S SENIORS ARE DIFFERENT FROM OTHER GENERATIONS

Baby boomers' view of when old age begins is very different from that of their parents. Boomers name eighty as the starting point of old age, compared to fifty-one for their parents. Many Boomers, unwilling to let life end at retirement, plan on starting a second career or owning a business when they retire and will continue to be active, interested, and involved as long as possible. As of 2000, 4.2 million (12.8 percent) Americans age sixty-five and over were still in the labor force, working or actively seeking work.

The educational level of the older population is also increasing. Between 1970 and 2000, the seniors who had completed high school rose from 28 percent to 70 percent, and in 2000 about 16 percent had a bachelor's degree or more. Research is revealing that exercising the mind keeps it fit and healthy just as physical exercise keeps the body fit and healthy, and lifelong learning improves the quality of life of the aging. *USA Today* reported that adults aged sixty-five and older spend over an hour and fifteen minutes a day reading–more than any other age group. Providing access to interesting, relevant and current materials and technology is a crucial element in helping seniors "use it or lose it." This audience will not be satisfied with a few large print books and a sing-a-long program. Libraries face the challenge of encouraging these educated, experienced, and active seniors to continue using the library by providing materials and services they will need and want.

SENIOR DEFINITIONS WILL CONTINUE TO CHANGE WORLDWIDE

The coming decades will see these trends grow exponentially as the Baby Boom generation enters retirement. People born during the early years of the baby boom, 1946 through 1950, fueled a 55 percent increase of the fifty- to fifty-four-year-old age group, the largest percentage growth between 1990 and 2000 of any five-year age group. The second fastest-growing group was the forty-five- to forty-nine-year-olds, which registered a 45 percent increase. This aging trend is also occurring in Australia, Canada, France, Germany, Japan, New Zealand, and the United Kingdom due to declining fertility rates, increasing longevity, and higher immigration rates.

WHO IS A "SENIOR ADULT"?

If we look at organizations serving seniors, we get several different answers to this question:

- AARP offers its membership to everyone age fifty and older, and their 55 Alive driving classes are for fifty-five and older.
- The corporate world defines their older workers at age forty-five and over, and the US census gives statistics for the older population as sixty-five and over.
- *The Statistical Abstract of the United States* says over 25 percent of the population is over fifty and 12.4 percent is over sixty-five.

When you consider this wide range of ages, it is clear that Chronological Age alone is not a good definition of who is a senior adult. From older workers approaching retirement in their fifties to the elderly in their eighties and nineties in nursing homes, there is a wide range of physical abilities, experiences, interests, and mental alertness represented, so no general definition based on these qualities will do either. The biological age that dictates our physical condition is different for everyone, and our Behavioral Age, or how old we act and think of ourselves, also affect our interests and needs. Expectations, cultural background, and economic life-style add even more variables that separate seniors into several stages of aging. See Figure 1-1.

THE SENIOR POPULATION IS DIVERSE

Along with the wide range in health and activity levels, the senior population is comprised of a great diversity of races and cultures. A large number of older immigrants are settling into industrialized countries and creating multicultural neighborhoods. In the United States, the African American, Asian, and Hispanic populations are expected to rise dramatically over the next two decades. Libraries have the special mission of not only providing these new citizens with information for living in a new country, but also educating everyone about the cultures represented in their communities. Libraries must provide many materials in

Figure 1-1 The National Health Interview Survey of the Non-institutionalized population tracked the subtle changes among the aging.	
Aged 50 to 54	79% live with spouse 74% in labor force 84% have good health 52% are women, 4% widowed 7% living below poverty level
Aged 55 to 59	65 % in labor force 81% health is good 52% are women 7 % widowed 7% living below poverty level
Aged 60 to 64	44% in labor force 75% have good health 54% are women, 13% widowed 8% living below poverty level
Aged 65 to 69	70% live with spouse 20% in labor force 75% have good health 55% are women 8% live below poverty level 10% live with relatives
Aged 70 to 74	61% live with spouse 10% in labor force 68% have good health 57% are women 11% living below poverty level
Aged 75 to 79	62% are women 50% live with spouse 6% in labor force 14% live below poverty level
Aged 80 to 84	40% live with spouse 63% have good health 64% are women, over 50% widowed 17% living below poverty level
Aged 85 and older	24% live with spouse 66% are women 63% have good health 17% living below poverty level 28% live with relatives

many different languages to meet the needs of the immigrant population; for example, the Queens Borough Public Library seeks to meet the needs of their large immigrant population by providing an online database directory of Immigrant-Serving Agencies in over fifty languages.

DEFINE THE LIBRARY'S ROLE IN SERVING SENIOR ADULTS

The American Library Association predicted the need for an increase of library services for the growing senior adult population. The ALA provided libraries with a set of seven guidelines for serving seniors. The *Library Services to Older Adults Guidelines*, www.ala.org/Content /NavigationMenu/RUSA/Professional_Tools4/Reference_Guidelines/ Library_Services_to_Older_Adults_Guidelines.htm are:

1. Integrate library service to older adults into the overall library plan, budget and service program.
2. Provide access to library buildings, materials, programs, and services for older adults.
3. Treat all older adults with respect at every service point.
4. Utilize the experience and expertise of older adults.
5. Provide and promote information and resources on aging.
6. Provide library services appropriate to the needs of older adults.
7. Collaborate with community agencies and groups serving older adults.

The ALA further encourages service to senior adults by offering the annual $1,000.00 Bessie Boehm Moore-Thorndike Press Award presented to a library that has developed an outstanding program for library service to the aging. The ALA's directive to serve older adults, our own library's mission statement goal of serving patrons of all ages, and the statistics telling us that our supporting, voting patrons are getting older indicates that libraries need to develop services, programs, and collections to meet their demands to remain a valuable and effective community contributor and resource. Librarians need to be trained to serve the older adult and departments must be developed to coordinate successful services similar to the flourishing children and young adult services.

When developing any new library service, you need a plan. Whether preparing a formal plan to present to library administration, or improving established services, there are key elements to consider.

ANSWER FIVE KEY PLANNING QUESTIONS

Marketing, funding, staffing, and publicity are the necessary building blocks that support library services and programs. To begin building a strong senior services department, we need to define and find the potential audience, learn what they want, decide how to provide what they want, and how to tell them when you have what they want. Start building your library's successful senior services on a firm foundation by finding the answers to five key planning questions:

- Who are today's seniors?
- Where are your seniors?
- What do your seniors want?
- How can you give your seniors what they want?
- How can you tell them you have what they want?

PLANNING QUESTION 1: WHO ARE YOUR SENIORS?

AREA AGENCY ON AGING

Your first task is defining and identifying the senior audience you plan to serve in your own community. Knowing their ages, ethnic background, and education will give you an idea of what kinds of programs may work in your library. Call or visit your Area Agency on Aging to find out what percentage of your community falls into the senior adult population, demographics, and information about services already offered to seniors in your area so you may supplement rather than duplicate services already in place. You can find where the nearest AAA is located at www.n4a.org/links.cfm. The library also may find a resource for speakers as shown in this list of a few of the many programs administered by our Region 9 AAA:

- Passport: provides in-home services for the frail low-income elderly
- Care Choice of Ohio: provides in home evaluation for long-term care options
- Adult Foster Home: residences providing accommodations, supervision and personal care
- Community Care Coordination: provides in-home care for those not eligible for Medicaid
- Training and Speakers Bureau: provides services and professionals available to speak on a variety of aging related topics
- Adult Day Care
- Legal Services
- Nutrition

US CENSUS

The latest US census reports at www.census.gov will allow you to look at the Quick Facts link for your state and county to see what percentage of your population is over sixty-five, their education level, race, and sex. Checking these resources and contacting local services will help you define the potential senior audience you want to reach. The Ohio State University Extension Office compiles statistics into profiles for each county of Ohio that include a breakdown of population into sex and race for five year age ranges.

DEMOGRAPHICS WORKSHEET

Our Demographics Worksheet in Figure 1-2 shows our library's geographical service area (Coshocton County): the total population is over 36,000 people, and according to the 2000 census, 14.7 percent are seniors. Keep a similar worksheet of your local statistics to apply for grants, justify the need for a program, and give you some tips on what kinds of programs may work for your audience. For example, our sheet shows there are 161 grandparents responsible for caring for their grandchildren. Can the library provide a service that would support them in their untraditional roles?

Figure 1-2 Worksheet: Coshocton County Senior Adult Population Demographics

Population Group	# of seniors		Source
Total county population	36, 655		US Census
Over 65	5, 172	14.7 %	
Female		51.2 %	
White		97.4 %	
African American		1.1 %	
Native American		.02 %	
Asian		.03 %	
Hispanic		.06 %	
Other		.02 %	
Age Range 50-54	2,360		Coshocton County Profiles
Age Range 55-59	1,812		
Age Range 60-64	1,599		
Age Range 65-69	1,398		
Age Range 70-74	1,440		
Age Range 75-79	1,156		
Age Range 80-84	787		
Age Range Over 85	635		
Grandparents responsible for grandchildren	161		US Census
65+ with a disability	2,217		

PLANNING QUESTION 2: WHERE ARE YOUR SENIORS?

OBSERVE YOUR LIBRARY PATRONS

First, observe the seniors already using your library. Are there particular times of the day when seniors visit with each other in the library? The morning Coffee Club programs evolved from the idea of providing this group a chance for interesting conversation and discussion on a variety of topics. Are grandparents visiting the children's room with their grandchildren? "Grand Time @ the Library" programs were created to give these grandparents caring for grandchildren a safe and fun learning experience together at the library.

CALL OUTSIDE AGENCIES

Look over the list of agencies serving seniors in your area from the AAA: senior centers, residences, nursing homes, adult day care, and any agencies providing homebound services, such as Meals on Wheels or visiting nurses. Also look in the Yellow Pages of the phone book for local senior facilities and services and under Home Health Care and call to ask for the population numbers. Most churches and synagogues have programs that serve their homebound members; contact the local Council of Churches and ask if they have data about the local homebound seniors or call a random selection of churches to get a guestimate of how many homebound seniors there may be. Many of these seniors are potential patrons for your services.

Figure 1-3 Worksheet: Coshocton County Senior Adult Residence Populations	
Senior Apartment Complexes: Riverside Tower Covington Square Seton Hall	99 40 40
Assisted Living Facilities: Windsorwood Place	44
Nursing Homes: Coshocton Health and Rehab Autumn Health Care West Lafayette Rehab and Nursing Center Extended Care Facility	72 60 50 61
Homebound: Meals on Wheels Interim Home Health Care	180 80
Senior Center (Provides meals and transportation to medical care)	40 daily 134 weekly

PLAN FOR TWO SEPARATE SERVICE AUDIENCES

As you discover who and where your seniors are, it will become apparent that you will need different kinds of services for two different populations: the seniors that can come to the library and the seniors that need the library to come to them. You will find programs and services for the first group in Part 1, "How to Bring Seniors into the Library," and for the second group in Part 2, "How to Deliver Library Service to Seniors Where They Live."

PLANNING QUESTION 3: WHAT DO YOUR SENIORS WANT?

Most seniors are relatively healthy and active, but even subtle changes in their health can change their needs for information. Most seniors will experience a loss of paid employment, loss of friends, relatives, and spouses, a diminished income, a change in sensory and physical abilities, and role changes, all of which change their needs for shelter, nutrition, and information. The library can provide needed information, education, and recreation for seniors through the stages of aging, and offer opportunities to create new friendships.

PROMOTE SUCCESSFUL AGING

While working to meet the needs of older adults, it is important to avoid the "illness model" or emphasizing what seniors can no longer do. The Census Bureau estimates only five to seven percent of older adults live in nursing homes and five percent more are homebound, which means almost ninety percent are leading active and independent lives. When planning programs, focus on their abilities and their new interests and respect their life experiences Growing older is a very personal and individual process and there are more exceptions than there are rules to aging.

The MacArthur Foundation sponsored a study that concluded that there are three indicators of successful aging: avoiding disease and disability, maintaining mental and physical function, and continuing engagement with life. Health and fitness, grandparenting, travel, finances, politics, recreational and social opportunities, and gardening are a few of the many interests libraries can address in providing materials and services for senior adults. The library can become a lifelong learning center providing the recreational, informational and technological needs of the community's seniors.

Accommodating an older patronage requires an awareness of physical barriers in the library and making changes to remove them. Assistive technology can make all of a library's resources accessible to all patrons. When health fails and seniors are no longer able to come to the library, the library can reach out by providing home and residential facilities services to continue providing the benefits of lifelong learning and the enjoyment of reading.

GET TO KNOW YOUR AUDIENCE

It is good marketing practice to know your audience and find out what they need to make the best use of your resources. There are several methods to get to know your senior audience, and libraries have frequently used a combination of focus groups and surveys to help develop new services and policies.

CREATE FOCUS GROUPS

A focus group is a moderated group discussion in which a moderator and six to ten participants from the target audience gather for a sixty to ninety minute guided discussion. A focus group will not give you a broad picture of your audience, but it can give you ideas and direction for building services from a patron's point of view. A focus group held in a nursing home with several residents can help you find out what services and materials they would find most helpful and entertaining. A focus group of seniors who come into the library can help you design a room for a senior collection. The basic steps to conduct a focus group are:

- Select a topic
- Develop questions
- Choose a moderator
- Select participants
- Recruit participants
- Refine logistics
- Contact and confirm the participants
- Conduct the focus group
- Analyze the findings

USE SURVEYS

In your surveys, ask a few demographic questions to help define your target audience further and focus on a fairly narrow topic, such as collection development or a specific service. For example, the Computer Training Survey in Figure 1-4 was published in a library newsletter that is available to all patrons to help develop new computer classes. Surveys should focus on a few topics since a long survey will take a lot of time to assess before you get any usable information. Surveys can be given to every senior that comes to the library, every resident in a nursing home, or every homebound patron to give feedback from a wider segment of the target population than a focus group. In addition, surveys and focus groups can be held at the library, at a senior center, at residential facilities, or through a homebound service such as Meals on Wheels. It is helpful to establish a rapport with the staff of senior facilities because you will be cooperating with them to conduct a survey or focus group at those sites.

ESTABLISH SENIOR ADVISORY BOARDS

Creating a Senior Advisory Board modeled on the very popular Teen Advisory Board may help your library develop services and a collection that better meets the needs of your community. An advisory group of senior library patrons can meet regularly to brainstorm program ideas and do volunteer work or the Friends group or the Coffee Club

---

Figure 1-4 Computer Training Survey

I am interested in taking computer training classes at the Coshocton Public Library.
I would prefer: (check one)
_____ Daytime classes _____Evening classes
I am interested in: (check all that apply)
_____Online library catalog training _____ Web email
_____ Introduction to the Internet _____ Evaluating Web sites

Name _____

Phone _____Age (optional) _____

Return to Coshocton Public Library 655 Main ST Coshocton, OH 43812

described in Chapter 3 may serve as an advisory board or focus group on an as-needed basis. Find out more about starting a Senior Advisory Board in Chapter 8, "Groom Great Volunteers."

Once you have generated ideas with the focus groups and advisory board and collected data from surveys, the next step is to develop new services to meet these needs. This manual contains program and service suggestions that have worked in libraries of various sizes that you can adapt and experiment with to fit your audience.

PROVIDE EVALUATIONS

Evaluate the services you offer to help you develop more effective programming. After each program, complete a Program Record form listing resources, special equipment, speaker contact information, statistics, and notes of any changes you would want to try if you offer the program again. Include statistics and expenses in your records to justify programs to the administration and to aid in requesting funds, applying for grants, planning future programs, and sharing your program experiences with other librarians.

Add quotes and notes from the audience to your reports to show how the programs are appreciated by the participants. Attendees may also be a good resource for new program ideas and know good speakers in the community for future programs. Feedback can be formal with a handout at the end of a program, but informal chat with the participants can provide much more useful information.

PLANNING QUESTION 4: HOW CAN YOU GIVE YOUR SENIORS WHAT THEY WANT?

Once you know your audience and what they want, look at your resources to see how you can provide the services they want. Funding programs and staffing services are two major issues facing libraries as budgets continue to be cut; however, the ALA encourages libraries to budget for older adult services. Investigate these sources to supplement the library's budget:

- State Library grants
- Federal grants
- Local foundation grants

Figure 1-5 Program Record Form

Coshocton Public Library
Program Record

Program Title: Medicare 101

Program intended for: Senior Adults/ Caregivers for Elderly

Date: June 26, 2003

Time: 7:00- 9:00 pm

Brief Description: Jon Hackathorn, a representative from the Ohio Senior Health Insurance Information Program (OSHIIP), presented a program on information about Medicare and explained the OSHIIP program. This program provides free health information and services to people with Medicare.

Promotion: (Mark all that apply):

 X Newspaper   X radio   X Advertiser   X newsletter   X flyers   X posters

Other: An interview with Jon Hackathorn was arranged with the WTNS talk show on Monday, June 23 at 9:00-9:30 am. The program was highlighted with the Summer Reading events in the main floor display case. Flyers were delivered to area nursing homes and assisted living facilities, the Senior Center and Home Health Care, as well as to homebound patrons.

Special Materials Required: Refreshments, books displayed and available for check-out pertaining to Medicare.

Number of people attending: 15

Staff members involved: Sara Mesaros

Evaluation: This was a very informative and worthwhile program. Those who attended were very appreciative for the opportunity to learn about OSHIIP and what the program has to offer.

Other Comments: Jon Hackathorn, the representative from OSHIIP, was pleased with the attendance and felt the program was well received. This presentation was free of charge.

- Friends of the Library
- Volunteers
- Partnerships
- Business grants and donations
- Awards

CONSIDER SERVICE OPTIONS

There are several options for providing most services, each requiring a different amount of staff time and financial investment. Don't give up on an idea because you are understaffed or there are no funds. Consider all the options:

Service Idea:	Possible Options:
Home	books-by-mail delivery by staff delivery by volunteers delivery by family, selected by librarian delivery by partnering agency
Service to Residential Facility	bookmobile stop lobby stop deposit collection delivered by staff deposit collection delivered by courier deposit collection picked up by facility
Programming	provide materials and plans, activity directors to present allow library staff to conduct the programs provide materials and plans, volunteers to present

PARTNER FOR BETTER SERVICE

As the senior adult retired population continues to grow, the provision of services to this group will pass along to the younger working generation and government agencies will be strained to provide the needed health care, housing, entertainment, and other social needs. This trend will continue for the next sixty years in all industrialized countries according to "Population Aging: A Comparison among Industrialized Countries." Free and low cost programs and services are essential, both to the seniors who may be unable to pay for needed services on fixed and limited incomes and also to the agencies that find themselves operating on more restricted budgets as the tax base falls on a smaller generation of workers. Partnerships with other agencies to share funds and workload, and training capable volunteers can help the library serve more of its senior adult community. Collaboration of efforts among agencies will be essential to the survival of these services. Libraries can support and complement the efforts of the community in meeting the needs of its seniors, while also providing information and resources for seniors seeking work and volunteer opportunities. Chapter 5 Partnering with Outside Agencies will help you get started. Any library of any size can take a step towards serving their seniors when they consider all the options!

PLANNING QUESTION 5: HOW CAN YOU TELL THEM YOU HAVE WHAT THEY WANT?

NOTIFY LOCAL MEDIA

Once you have developed a wonderful service or program, you can notify your audience with these free or nearly free publicity ideas to reach seniors:

- Local radio and cable stations may offer free public service announcements, a traditional and free or inexpensive way to inform seniors about programs and services.

- Local newspapers will often publish a community calendar or area briefs that will announce current events of interest to seniors at no charge.

- A senior page can be created on the library's Web site to explain services and announce programs to Web-savvy seniors.

CREATE PRINTED PUBLICITY

Inform your current patrons who may have senior friends, neighbors, and relatives by including program information in flyers, the library newsletter, posters in elevators and near popular collections, and eye-catching collection displays. Distribute flyers and posters to senior facilities, churches, synagogues, funeral homes, beauty and barber shops, grocery stores, Laundromats, and doctors' offices. A few samples of flyers, bookmarks, posters and door hangers are included in this manual as samples. Tips for printed publicity:

- A large type size such as twelve point and a font that is not too ornate make reading easier.
- High gloss paper causes reflections that can make reading difficult.
- Ink and paper colors should contrast sharply. Black on yellow is the most readable from a distance.
- Reds, oranges, and yellows are more appealing to aging eyes than blues, greens, and purples.
- Use familiar images and a layout that flows easily.

USE A PERSONAL TOUCH

Develop working relationships with the Activity Directors of area senior facilities, send personal invitations to programs when appropriate, use door hangers in apartment buildings to announce services and programs, and speak about your services and programs at civic club meetings. Word of mouth is always your best publicity, so tell your seniors what is happening at the library for them, and they will pass it on.

BUILD ON THIS FOUNDATION

Serving Seniors: A How-To-Do-It Manual for Librarians will help your library develop services for the senior population in your community, keeping the ALA's guidelines in mind. Some libraries are accomplishing a few of these services through an outreach department that also encompasses the bookmobile service and service to other populations. Others provide occasional events for the general adult audience and seniors sometimes participate. Libraries planning for the future are developing Senior Services Departments that focus on all the services

Figure 1-6 Senior Services Flyer

the library can provide for senior adults that are as comprehensive and active as the children's and young adult departments.

This manual—a collection of programs, services, and resources that have worked in many libraries in the United States and Canada—is meant to inspire more libraries to create and expand programming for their lifetime readers, often the very people who established and supported these same libraries and will continue to support them with their patronage, votes, taxes and volunteer efforts.

RESOURCES:

1. Smith, Olivia J., ed. 2000. *Aging in America*. New York: H. W. Wilson.

2. Walker, Michael C. 2002. *Marketing to Seniors*. Bloomington, IN: 1st Books Library.

3. Anderson, Gerard F. and Peter Sotir Hussey. 2000. "Population Aging: A Comparison among Industrialized Countries." *Health Affairs* 19, no. 3 (May 1): 191.

4. Bryan, Carol. "Help Seniors Respond to Your Printed Message." *Library Imagination Paper* 22, no. 3 (Summer 2000): 1.

5. Kleiman, Allan M. "The Aging Agenda." *Library Journal* 120, no. 7 (April 15, 1995): 32-35.

6. Kotulak, Ronald. 1996. "Keeping the Brain Sharp as We Age." *Saturday Evening Post* 268, no. 6 (November): 50-56.

7. Pol, Louis G. 1992. "Eight Stages of Aging." *American Demographics* 14, no. 8 (August): 54.

8. Tangley, Laura. 2000. "Aging Brains Need Fresh Challenges to Stay Agile." *U.S. News & World Report* 52 (June 5): 90.

9. Trafford, Abigail. 2002. "Keeping the Grow in Growing Old: At Chatauqua, Seniors Gather to Exercise Their Minds, Stay Sharp and Keep Themselves Moving Forward." *Washington Post*, October 15: HE01.

10. Administration on Aging. "A Profile of Older Americans: 2002: Future Growth." www.aoa.gov/prof/Statistics/profile/profiles2002.asp.

11. Ohio State University Extension. "Coshocton County Profile." www.ag.ohio-state.edu/~dataunit/profiles/cosh.html.

12. SeniorJournal.com. "Senior Citizen Stats." www.seniorjournal.com/SeniorStats.htm.

13. National Association of Area Agencies on Aging. "N4A Links." www.n4a.org/links.cfm.

14. U.S. Census Bureau: United States Department of Commerce. "The Statistical Abstract of the United States." www.census.gov/prod/www/statistical-abstract-us.html.

15. US Census Bureau. "The Older Population in the United States: March 2000 Detailed Tables" www.census.gov/population/www/socdemo/age/ppl-147.html.

16. U. S. Census Bureau: United States Department of Commerce. "United States Census 2000." www.census.gov.

2 BUILD A COLLECTION TO SERVE SENIOR ADULTS

Libraries are not made; they grow.

—Augustine Birrell

OVERVIEW

Seniors have a more diverse taste in reading material than any other age group due to their vast differences in experiences, lifestyles, and interests over their lifetimes. Topics they may not have read about before are suddenly very important: income and investments, health and insurance issues, and housing and care choices, for example, not only for themselves, but for their aging parents.

All of these collections need to be up to date to be useful, so a first step is to evaluate, weed, and update the collection with the senior audience in mind. Every good fiction collection also needs to be weeded periodically to make room for new titles, and the withdrawn large print and audio fiction materials in good condition are welcome free gifts for the home libraries of residential facilities.

Specific subject areas to update are:

- Income and Investments
- Retirement
- Health and Insurance Issues
- Grandparenting
- Housing and Long Term Care Options
- Starting Small Businesses
- Antiques and Collectibles
- Fashion and Skin Care for Older Women
- Relationships for Older Couples
- Cooking for One or Two and Special Diet Cookbooks
- Prescription Drug Information
- Multicultural Materials relevant to your community

A few libraries are creating Senior Spaces where many of the materials that meet this group's special needs are available in one area. Include multimedia kits, large print books and magazines, games, videos and audio materials to assist activity professionals, caregivers and volunteers who work with seniors. Make this space senior friendly with good lighting and seating that isn't hard to get out of! The catalog and the collection need to be wheel chair and walker accessible, with wider aisles and shelves that are not too high or too low. High and low shelves are not only difficult to reach; they are hard to read with bifocal lenses. Place stools at the ends of aisles so patrons can stop a moment to rest and browse.

Create a Senior Information Center in this space to house pamphlets and flyers on health issues, financial information, local, state, and federal services for seniors, and educational and recreational opportunities in the community. Contact area agencies and ask them to provide their brochures for the center; agencies are often happy to do so because they reach even more seniors with no extra mailing or market research expense. The seniors benefit by having all the information in one place, and the library benefits by adding value to the services it provides to seniors.

Figure 2-1 Collect brochures from area agencies that serve seniors to create a Senior Information Center.

New materials help ease the difficulties caused by some common physical changes in seniors. For patrons who wear bifocal lenses for reading, books in large print and audio formats can be more relaxing and enjoyable. While larger print means larger, heavier books, many companies are publishing their large print materials in soft covers, which is a real consideration for patrons who have arthritic hands. Descriptive and captioned videos make movies accessible to patrons with more severe vision and hearing loss.

A few companies have put together kits that make programming for seniors an easier task for librarians and activity directors and can be used as models to create program theme kits on any topic.

Some book companies are leasing large print and audio materials, which helps library funds for special collections go farther and solves storage issues. Adaptive technology in libraries improves accessibility for all patrons with disabilities, including our senior adult audience. These assistive technologies are some of the things that libraries need (along with large print, audio books, etc) to make their collections more accessible.

LARGE PRINT MATERIALS

Large print books and magazines are the most common and most appreciated special collections for seniors in public libraries. The Lighthouse National Survey on Vision Loss reported one in six Americans over the age of forty-five have trouble reading small print. Soft cover editions of large print books circulate much better when they are available since the larger print can make a good long novel heavy and cumbersome for arthritic hands or for reading comfortably in bed, and longer novels may be more enjoyable in an audio format.

The *Complete Directory of Large Print Books and Serials* is a subject, author, title, periodical, and newspaper index to publications available in large print with a list of publishers and services. Thorndike Press, which emphasizes bestsellers and genre fiction, is currently the number one large print publisher with over 900 titles a year and also publishes large print in Spanish. Random House offers a full-line of best-selling fiction and nonfiction titles in hardcover and at the same price as the trade editions. *New York Times Large Print Weekly* is condensed from each week's *New York Times* and *Reader's Digest* has a monthly large print condensed version of its popular periodical. Published quarterly, The *Large Print Literary Reader* reprints several classic stories in each soft cover edition.

LARGE PRINT BOOKS FOR LEASE

The advantages of leasing large print books are a lower cost per circulation and the ability to return books with a short shelf life. For example, while patrons will receive their requested bestseller title faster if there are multiple copies, the library may not want to fund the purchase of many copies of the same title and dedicate the shelf space to them when the demand is over. If leased, the duplicate copies can be returned when no longer needed. Leasing is also helpful when storage for special collections is limited. Rather than storing a book that is no longer circulating, it is returned to the lease company. Patrons not only get to read their bestsellers sooner, but leased materials often arrive long before the same title is acquired from the regular distributors. Leasing may be a sensible alternative for your library when funds and space are limited for large print collections.

MAGAZINES

Seniors read all kinds of magazines, but some magazines are published specifically for the senior audience. *Reminisce* and *Good Old Days* accept submissions from their readers, so the stories, photos, and articles are personal and interesting to read. *Ideals* has inspirational, touching, and amusing short stories and poems and colorful photographs. *AARP: the Magazine*, formerly *Modern Maturity*, available in print and online, covers a wide range of topics, including health, work, entertainment, and travel. *Guideposts*, a publication of personal inspirational stories, also comes in large print. These magazines can be good sources for poems and stories for programs and are attractive for browsing.

AUDIO BOOKS AND BRAILLE MATERIALS

Libraries are expanding their audio collections to meet the demands of patrons of all ages. Audio books on tape and CD are perfect not only for those experiencing failing eyesight or eyestrain, but also for travelers and anyone who enjoys listening to a story while cooking, cleaning, or working on other projects. Audio materials are also helpful to those that learn better by listening than reading. Tapes and CDs of radio programs, music, short stories, and humor can also be used during programs for seniors.

The National Library Service for the Blind and Physically Handicapped of the Library of Congress (www.loc.gov/nls) provides audio books and magazines and Braille materials free of charge to eligible patrons. The Talking Books program, available in every state of the US, allows legally blind, visually or physically handicapped, or learning disabled patrons to receive talking books, playback equipment and Braille books by mail from regional libraries. Local libraries can house the equipment for loan, distribute literature about the service, provide applications, deliver machines, make referrals and provide additional titles from their own collections. Contact your state library to be included in the Talking Books program.

VIDEOS

Sight-impaired seniors can enjoy films by using descriptive videos and hearing-impaired patrons can enjoy captioned videos. The descriptive videos provide a narration of the key visual elements in the program including actions, costumes, gestures and scene changes. Captioned videos identify speakers and display dialog in print on the screen, and often describe sound effects and music. The Descriptive Video Service produces captioned and descriptive videos in VHS and DVD formats and also captions software.

PROGRAM KITS

BiFolkal Productions offers kits of packaged resources and ideas for reminiscence programs. Topics available include: County Fairs, Train Rides, 1924, School Days, The Depression, Farm Days, Fall, Automobiles, Birthdays, Summertime, Home Front, Work Life, Fashion, Music, Fun and Games, Pets, Home, African American Lives, The Fifties, and Spring. The kits, meant to create programs that stimulate the senses and help seniors recall and share their memories, include slide carousels, videos, audio tapes, large print booklets, suggestions for activities, large print skit scripts, props, and a leader's manual. BiFolkal Kits cost $300.00 each, but Mini-Kits and parts of kits can be purchased separately. While these kits are relatively expensive, a consortium can invest in them and rotate the collection among member libraries, or branch libraries can borrow them from a central location. Librarians can use the kits to present programs or they may be loaned to activity directors of residential facilities to do their own programming. BiFolkal also produces Actiphile kits and Slideas slide sets. Actiphile kits, priced at $20.00 per file, include files of a dozen or more holiday activities with skits, recipes, songs, poems, craft ideas, quizzes, and word puzzles that may be photocopied. Slideas Slide Sets, at a cost of $25.00 each, include twenty slides, a guide, discussion questions, suggested activities and a resource guide.

Figure 2-2 "Remembering Summertime" from BiFolkal Productions will help elderly seniors recall the summer activities of their youth.

ElderSong Publications is a publisher and distributor of over 150 books, videos, and recordings for activities coordinators, recreation and creative arts therapists, occupational and rehab therapists, and other caregivers who work with older adults. ElderSong also offers a nice selection of games, songs, videos, and books that will interest both the men and the women in your audiences.

Eldergames stimulates reminiscing by offering games, activities kits, and materials for the elderly. Inexpensive and versatile, the materials can supplement library materials to make hands-on programs.

Create a paper or computer file of program ideas and list the materials the library already owns with Web sites that would be helpful for each program. This file is an easy and fast resource when you need a program idea at the last minute or an activity director needs program materials in a hurry. Print out the list and collect the items in a bag or basket for checkout. A file of cards takes less space to store than assembled kits and the materials can remain on the shelves available for other patrons. A generous list of resources allows for items that may be checked out already.

You can pre-package these items into theme kits, ready for check-out, if there is space to store them. Theme kits may include books, an audio tape, a video, posters or photo cards, and realia objects. A durable container that stores easily, like storage tubs that stack, work well. Include a price list of the items in the kit so the user can be sure to return everything and add a complete list of the kit contents to the catalog record. It is helpful to allow activity directors to reserve the kits so they may plan their programs.

LIBRARY WEB SITES

The library's Web site can include a page dedicated to seniors that is easy to navigate, written in a large font, and without too many bells and whistles for seniors new to the Internet. Pages that load quickly, have a similar style throughout the site, and have an internal search engine will also be easier to use. A successful senior web page will list library programs and services for seniors, special collections, and a selection of annotated links to interesting and helpful sites. Include a feedback e-mail link to make it easy to ask a question, and add a link to the catalog with instructions for placing holds. Distribute large print bookmarks with the page's URL for home use at every program and through outreach services. Ask the PR department to do a feature article in the newsletter. More tips from the SPRY Foundation for creating a Web page for senior adults can be found at www.spry.org/pdf/website_creators_guide.pdf. Check the list of library sites for seniors in Appendix D for inspiration to build your own.

ASSISTIVE TECHNOLOGY

Technology—from basic magnifying glasses to screen reading software—has made information more accessible for all patrons. Since some of this equipment can be expensive, civic organizations such as the Lions Club or the Rotary, may want to help the library make a purchase to assist senior adults and other patrons with physical restrictions.

Magnifying equipment at the library can make any material more readable. Making magnifying glasses and page-sized magnifying sheets available at the reference desk will make reading phone books, dictionaries, and other reference materials easier. Some libraries may have the funding to make these items available for checkout. Photocopiers that have enlarging capabilities can reprint the small print of contracts, instructions, and documents to make them easier for seniors to read.

A CCTV, closed-circuit television, uses a video camera to project a magnified image in a monitor. The price of the unit depends on options like zoom lenses, stand cameras, hand held cameras, and color or black and white monitors. Some computer-compatible cameras allow users to magnify an object on the monitor by placing it in front of the camera. This equipment, ranging in price from $400–$4000, is useful for reading any printed material, and some models have room under the camera to allow for writing as well. Software programs like MAGic®, with a standard-edition price of $545, magnify a computer screen and offer a speech option.

Two competitive text-to-speech machines are the Kurzweil Reading Machine and Open Book by Freedom Scientific, ranging in price from $350–$2700. The Kurzweil Company invented the first of the text-to-speech synthesizers, which utilize a scanner and an optical recognition program that translates the scanned material into words that are read to the user by a synthesized voice. Today's machines can read and record the written as well as printed text in several languages and have many features compatible with computers. Headphones keep the material private for the patron. See the resources for a good online article comparing the two machines. A similar product, JAWS for Windows, uses a screen-to-speech synthesizer and sound card to provide access to computer software and the Internet to those with vision loss. A sixty day trial version costs $40.00 and the software runs about $1200.00.

RESOURCES

FOR LARGE PRINT BOOKS AND MAGAZINES:

1. The Complete Directory of Large Print Books and Serials, 2002. New Providence, NJ: R.R. Bowker.

2. Elder-berries: Library Programs for Older Adults. 1998. 2nd ed. Columbus, OH: Ohio Library Council.

3. Daily Guideposts. "Guideposts Store." www.dailyguide posts.com/cgi-bin/sgdynamo.exe?HTNAME=_magstand.htm.

4. Caviness, Rochelle. "Large Print Reviews." www.largeprint reviews.com/lpmags.html.

5. "Large Print Literary Reader Magazine Subscriptions." www.4magazines.net/lplr-4.html.

6. "NYT Large Print Weekly Magazine Subscriptions." www.4mag azines.net/nylp-26.html.

7. "Random House Large Print." www.randomhouse.com/largeprint/index.html.

8. "Reader's Digest Large Print for Easier Reading." www.rd.com/rd1/ms/rdlp/rdlp_issue.jsp?trkid=pubalt_rdlp.

9. Thomson Gale. "Thorndike Press." www.galegroup.com/thorndike.

FOR LEASING BOOKS:

1. Brodart. "McNaughton Adult Book Service Plans." http://divisions.brodart.com/books/mcn/adltbook.htm.

FOR MAGAZINES:

1. "Elderhostel Catalog." www.elderhostel.org.

2. "Good Old Days Online." "House of White Birches." www.goodolddaysonline.com/pages/magazines.html.

3. AARP. "AARP: The Magazine." www.aarpmagazine.org.

4. Reiman Publications. "Reminisce: the Magazine That Brings Back the Good Times." https://commerce.cdsfulfillment.com/REM/subscriptions.cgi.

FOR AUDIO:

1. "Audio Editions: Books on Cassette and CD." www.audioeditions.com.

2. "Books on Tape: Unabridged Audiobooks and More." http://library.booksontape.com.

3. "Brilliance Audio." www.brillianceaudio.com.

4. Library of Congress National Library Service for the Blind and Physically Handicapped (NLS). "That All May Read…" www.loc.gov/nls.

5. Recorded Books. "What's New for Libraries." www.recordedbooks.com/library/index.cfm.

6. MediaBay, Inc. "Your Source for Spoken Word Audio." www.mediabay.com.

FOR VIDEOS:

1. Sentimental Productions. "America's Delightful Past in Story and Song on Video." www.sentimental.cc.

2. Media Access Group at WGBH. "DVS® Services." http://main.wgbh.org/wgbh/pages/mag/services/description.

3. Terra Nova Films. "Videos on Aging." www.terranova.org.

FOR BRAILLE MATERIALS:

1. Braille Institute. "Library Services Links." www.braille library.org/ Serv-Lib-Links.html.

2. Enabling Technologies. "Braille Printers from Enabling Technologies." www.brailler.com.

FOR PROGRAM KITS:

1. Bi-Folkal Productions, Inc. "Welcome to Bi-Folkal!" www.bifol kal.org.

2. Eldersong Publications, Inc. "Your Source for Creative Activity Materials for Older Adults." www.eldersong.com.

3. National Council on Aging. "Order Form: Eldergames." https://www.ncoa.org/content.cfm?sectionID=30.

FOR CCTV:

1. ABLEDATA. "ABLEDATA: Explore the World of Assistive Technology." www.abledata.com/Site_2/Default.htm.

2. American Foundation for the Blind. "Video Magnifiers." www.afb.org/info_document_view.asp?documentid=221.

FOR READING MACHINES AND SCREEN MAGNIFIERS:

1. Andrews, David. "Comparing the Open Book and the Kurzweil 1000." The Braille Monitor. www.nfb.org/Bm/Bm01/Bm0102/bm010210.htm.

2. Ai Squared. "Computer Access Solutions for the Visually Impaired." www.aisquared.com.

3. Freedom Scientific. "Software." www.freedomscientific.com/fs_products/software.asp.

4. G.W. Micro. "Window Eyes 4.5." www.gwmicro.com.

5. Kurzweil Educational Systems. "Products and Services." www.kurzweiledu.com/products.asp.

3 START A DISCUSSION GROUP

The test and the use of man's education is that he finds pleasure in the exercise of his mind.

—Jacques Martin Barzun

OVERVIEW

Discussions are interesting and stimulating programs. They provide enjoyable social interaction and exposure to new ideas and topics for the participants. The discussion programs in this chapter utilize the library's collection and offer a neutral meeting place at the library. An appreciation of thc arts and literature can be expressed in these lively discussion groups. Many libraries have found that morning and afternoon programs are better attended since seniors often do not like to drive after dark. You can guide these discussions yourself by researching the topic beforehand, but plan to allow plenty of time for the group members to contribute. Invite an occasional speaker to introduce a topic, but once again, leave time for the discussion and questions. Always display library materials that support the topic at the program and create bookmarks or handouts with resources so patrons can pursue more information at a later date. Light refreshments help create a friendly and conversational atmosphere.

BOOK DISCUSSION GROUPS

Books are the quietest and most constant of friends;
They are the most accessible and wisest of counselors,
And the most patient of teachers.

—Charles W. Eliot

A book discussion is a time-tested program for many libraries, and seniors enjoy them, too. It is important to offer books in a variety of formats to include patrons who may need large print or audio versions of the selected title. Choose titles several months ahead to allow patrons time to reserve or purchase and read materials. Establish the meetings for the same day each month and plan on one and a half hours for a good discussion. Arrange tables and chairs so the participants will be facing each other by pushing tables together and arranging the chairs around the perimeter. The discussion leader sits with the group.

Prepare for the discussion by reading the book and making notes with an overall description of the theme, plot, characters, setting, and background information about the author. Begin the meeting with introductions and nametags to help everyone get to know each other. As you get to know your group, you will discover some members may tend to dominate and others may be reluctant to speak; keep the discussion on track by maintaining a balance between personal revelations and reactions to the book. Prepare questions in case discussion slows down and use them to move on when someone ventures too far away from the topic.

Select books that have substance, generate enthusiasm, and offer intellectual growth for the most interesting, thought provoking discussions. Check the resources at the end of the chapter for helpful tips to get a group started, lead a group, and select books to discuss. Offer coffee, tea and cookies as easy refreshments.

FILM DISCUSSION GROUPS

More than a movie night, film discussion groups offer seniors a social outing with conversation about a common film interest. Home theatre equipment and a big screen television for good sound and easy viewing make the films more enjoyable, but a VCR or DVD player with a video projector and screen will work also, and some libraries still have access to 16 mm films and projectors. Renting the equipment for occasional events is an option if there are no funds for purchase. Unless you are showing films that have public performance rights, your library will need to acquire a movie license from a licensing company who will provide a list of the films covered by the license. Show excerpts from the films and encourage discussion throughout. Book and video/DVD displays at the program encourage browsing and checkouts. One to one and a half hours is the average length for these programs and morning or afternoons will attract more seniors. Popcorn is appropriate as a movie snack.

REEL TALK

Do you know patrons of the library that are movie fans and collectors of memorabilia? Invite these film buffs to lead a series of classic film discussions. The speaker can share his passion for his favorite film by sharing trivia, showing his collection of movie posters and memorabilia, and commenting on excerpts from the film. One movie can be featured at each of the discussion meetings. Suggested films are *It Happened One Night, Shane, White Christmas, Yankee Doodle Dandy, Roberta, Mr. Smith Goes to Washington, The Jolson Story*, and *Casablanca*. Display books about the actors and the movies and more films in the same genre.

HOW THE WEST WAS OR WASN'T

Several film discussion program ideas are offered in the Ohio Library Council publication *Elder-Berries*. "How the West Was or Wasn't" is a two part discussion series comparing Hollywood's version and the historical version of the Old West. Show excerpts from classic western films and a television western in the first session and invite discussion throughout. Suggested films are *Iola's Promise, Big Trail, My Darling Clementine, Shane, High Noon* and *Roy Rogers*. Focus on the reality of the hardships for those that traveled west in the second session by showing excerpts from *The Real West* and *Gone West*. Display books on the West and westerns on video and DVD for browsing and checkout.

HOLLYWOOD HEARTTHROBS

"Hollywood Heartthrobs," another film discussion program from *Elder-Berries*, focuses on favorite movie stars from the old days with excerpts from films such as Mae West's *I'm No Angel* and Douglas Fairbank's *Thief of Baghdad*. Feature biographies of movie stars and movie history books. Other film discussion themes to try are silent films and classic villains. Similarly, try a discussion about radio comedians based on the films *Great Radio Comedians: Parts I, II,* and *III*. Browse your library's 16 mm film collection and video/DVD collection for more ideas.

FOREIGN FILMS

Foreign film showings will be enjoyed by foreign film buffs and immigrant patrons. The films can inspire discussion, a sharing of experiences, and connection with the multicultural community. English subtitled films will attract a wider audience. Visit On Video at www.onvideo.org/re_for.htm for a list of foreign film resources and catalogs.

COFFEE CLUB AT THE LIBRARY

Good communication is as stimulating as black coffee and just as hard to sleep after.

—Anne Morrow Lindbergh

Invite seniors to start a Coffee Club with a different discussion topic every month. Schedule the meetings for one morning a month and plan on about two hours for most discussions. Make nametags for everyone; send a post card reminder a week before the meeting, and a core group should form after a few meetings. An average of fourteen to sixteen can gather around four long tables pushed together to make one large table. Display library materials on the month's discussion topic with library newsletters and program flyers on another table. Serve fresh ground coffee to make it special and place refreshments on platters to pass around the table. Decorate the tables simply, use paper goods that suit the season or theme, and place notepaper, a pencil, and a bookmark at each place setting. Research the topic so you may begin the discussion and get it going again if conversation lapses. Announce the topic for the next month so group members can bring books or other "show and tell" items to add to the discussion. Occasionally invite a guest to speak, but always allow time for questions and discussion.

Figure 3-1 Include the topic of discussion for the next meeting on postcard reminders to the Coffee Club members.

You are invited to join
The Coffee Club
at the Coshocton Public Library

on January 13, 2003 at 10:00 am.
We will meet in the large meeting room
for a cup of hot coffee and lively conversation.
The topic for this month is
New Books for the New Year

Coffee Club is a great forum for discussions of holidays and commemorative events, allowing seniors to learn and share cultural history. Figure 3-6 lists many holidays that will inspire interesting and educational discussions. All the discussions follow a similar format: share a bit of historical background, share photos and props, and display books and materials on the topic. The coffee club members will do the rest!

JANUARY: NEW BOOKS FOR THE NEW YEAR/FRUGAL LIVING

The things I want to know are in books; my best friend is the man who'll get me a book I ain't read.

—Abraham Lincoln

"Pass It On" is a book review activity for the Coffee Club. Gather several newly processed books to present to the group for a first look. Explain what they will need to look for in the books: read the front inside cover and the information about the author on the back inside cover. How much research did the author do for the book, is it based on fact? What catches their attention about this book? Check the table of contents; does it sound interesting? Distribute the new books, one to each member, to look over for three minutes and then pass to his neighbor on the right. He then looks at the book for three minutes, and so on until everyone has looked at three different books. You can watch the clock or set a timer and join in the book review. The guests then talk about the books they reviewed, sharing a bit about each book, whether they would like to read them and why or why not. Offer the books for checkout at the end of the meeting. Check the library display supplies for snowmen or snowflakes to decorate the table and make or purchase bookmarks that say "Warm up with a good book!" Add a winter clip art image to plain paper for the notepaper. Serve citrus fruit and coffee cake.

After the holidays, everyone tightens his or her belt, so glean tips on frugal living from "Cheapskate Monthly" and *Tightwad Gazette* and ask the group to share their best tips for frugal living. Check out the Web site and book in the resources for advice on getting out of debt, figuring interest rates, and even cooking frugal recipes.

FEBRUARY: LIBRARY TOUR SCAVENGER HUNT/VALENTINES DAY/BLACK HISTORY MONTH

A tour of the library is always an interesting activity for patrons because it allows them to see behind the scenes, meet library staff, and

Figure 3-2 Coffee Club members get the first peek at new books in the Pass It On book review.

explore collections they might not have been aware of before. A scavenger hunt makes the tour even more interesting by turning it into a hands-on activity. To create this simple scavenger hunt, first write down the rooms the group will be touring in the order they will be visited, leaving the room where you are meeting for last. Write a question about something in each of the rooms, choosing things that would be of particular interest to seniors so they will learn where some helpful resources are located. Print a copy of the hunt for each group member and provide pencils. During the tour, be sure to include a hint about the answer while talking about the room and allow time for chatting, questions and discovery. When the tour and hunt conclude in the meeting room, reward the players with a library bag of handouts, bookmarks, library pencils, magnets, and other free items your library offers. Over coffee and refreshments, lead the group in a discussion of what they learned about the library.

Decorate for Valentine's Day and place bookmarks of the Dewey Decimal system and notepaper with a library quote at each place setting of the discussion table. Serve Valentine cookies and cinnamon candy hearts for refreshments.

Tomorrow is St Valentine's Day
All in the morning betime,

And I a maid at your window,
To be your valentine!

—William Shakespeare in *Hamlet*

History and trivia about Valentine's Day will inspire a sharing of Valentine memories for your Coffee Club. Invite members to bring keepsake candy boxes, valentines, or other memorabilia from past Valentine Days to share. Place bookmarks and note paper with a Valentine quote at each seat and serve cupcakes decorated with conversation heart candies and peanuts with the coffee.

Bringing the gifts that my ancestors gave,
I am the dream and the hope of the slave.
I rise
I rise
I rise.

—Maya Angelou (1928–)

Present the historical background of Black History Month to begin a discussion of the contributions of famous Black Americans. When the celebration of Black History Month began in 1926 as "Negro History Month"," little was known about the history of African Americans, although they had been in America since colonial times. We owe the celebration and the study of black history to Dr. Carter G. Woodson, and February was chosen as the month to celebrate because it marks the birthdays of Abraham Lincoln and Frederick Douglas, who greatly impacted the American black population. Prepare for the discussion with photographs of famous and not-so-famous Black Americans and trivia questions to inspire more discussion.

Hand out bookmarks with a list of famous black Americans and quotes, a crossword, or a word search puzzle.

MARCH: ST. PATRICK'S DAY

May your heart be warm and happy
With the lilt of Irish laughter
Every day in every way
And forever and ever after!

—*Irish Blessing*

Begin a discussion of Irish heritage and travels to Ireland with a short history of Saint Patrick and a bit o' Irish trivia. Read a few Irish blessings and display books about Ireland, set in Ireland, or by Irish authors for browsing, discussion and checkout. Invite members to talk about their Irish heritage or travels to Ireland, decorate with shamrocks, and add bookmarks and notepaper with Irish blessings for each place setting. Serve green refreshments: kiwi and green frosted cookies with Irish Cream cappuccino.

APRIL: NATIONAL POETRY MONTH/GARDENING

Ask members to bring their favorite poems to share for "Poetry Through the Ages." Create a display explaining National Poetry Month with poetry books to browse and check out. A low vase of fresh spring flowers on the table will look cheery. Add spring bookmarks and notepaper at each place setting and serve pineapple and a light pastry.

Compose a group poem using a writing activity adapted from *Elder-Berries*. Use one flip chart or dry erase board to list words the audience generates, and use a second to compose the poem. Choose a main subject for the poem, such as "spring." To generate the five lines of this "cinquain," ask the audience to:

- Suggest nouns relating to spring, write them on the first chart, and choose the best one to be the first line of the poem on the second chart.

- Suggest words ending in –y or –ly to describe the first line, write them on the first chart, and choose two of the words to be the second line of the poem on your second chart.

- Suggest words ending in –ing to describe the first line and write them on the first chart, choose three of the words, and write them as the third line of the poem on the second chart.

- Complete the phrase, "as _____ as _____" to describe the first line, choose the best one from the group's suggestions, and write this on your second chart as the fourth line of the poem.

- Suggest words that are synonyms for the word on the first line, choose one, and write it on the second chart as the final line of the poem.

"Daffodils" is an example of a poem written this way. Create springtime bookmarks with the new poem on them to pass out at the main desk for National Poetry Month. Great publicity for the Coffee Club!

Daffodils
Cheerily, brightly
Nodding, waving, welcoming
As breezy as spring
Yellow sunshine.

Gardening is a popular pastime, and April is a good time to share gardening tips and expertise. Display vegetable and flower gardening books and videos, prepare a list of gardening tips and advice to share with the group, and decorate with a basket of ceramic or wooden vegetables or a fresh pot of herbs. If you prefer, turn to the pros and invite a master gardener to speak and answer questions about new equipment and methods for senior gardeners. Provide notepaper with a gardening verse and a spring bookmark And serve small bagels with vegetable cream cheese and fresh fruit.

MAY: TEA

For this meeting, share the history of tea, give lessons on reading tealeaves, or invite a guest speaker from the local museum to share the history of tea and a collection of antique teapots. Allow time for questions and discussion. Decorate with flowery and lacey paper goods, offer several teas, and serve fresh fruit and cream cheese sandwiches.

JUNE: ROSES/SUMMER READS

Some people are always grumbling because roses have thorns. I am thankful that thorns have roses.

—Alphonse Karr

For a discussion about roses, ask if there are rose gardeners in the group and share rose trivia and rose quotes. A poster game, "A Rose by Any Other Name" asks players to match names with roses. Scan and paste photos of roses with literary names on a poster: William Shakespeare, Canterbury, Redcoat, Chaucer, The Nun, Wise Portia, and Sweet Julia. If you have a source of free rose petals, make rose potpourri and rose water to give to each member with the recipes. Decorate the table with roses or rose petals and serve small bagels with strawberry cream cheese and fresh strawberries.

If your group would rather discuss light summer reads, play the "Pass It On" game described for January. Pass around new novels that would make great beach books and talk about the summer reading programs and any other special events and activities at the library. Share

---

Figure 3-3 Rose potpourri and rosewater are beautiful and thoughtful gifts for your Coffee Club members and cost very little to make.

Rose Potpourri

Collect petals from the rose as the flower reaches fully open maturity, but before it turns brown. Dry them until crisp on a screen, cookie sheet or any flat surface. Red roses, when dried, turn a rich burgundy color and look lovely in a ginger jar, candy dish or antique canister.

For each quart of petals, add 1 tablespoon dry lavender (fixative), 1 tablespoon cloves (complementary spice). Add a few drops of essential oil (aroma fixative) or your favorite perfume.

Seal your potpourri mixture in a jar to mellow for approximately 10 days.

To properly blend the ingredients, shake the jar lightly every couple of days.

Rose Water

Put 3 large handfuls of fresh red rose petals into a clean pot.

Pour one liter distilled water over the rose petals

Cover the pot and place it over low heat. Let simmer until half the water is left.

Let cool.

Discard the petals and pour the liquid (rosewater) into a sterile bottle.

---

what the children and teens are reading along with the summer reading program statistics. Serve melon and sugar cookies.

JULY: APRONS/SUMMERTIME FUN

You can create a program by building your discussion around a collection. For example, in our library an apron collection spanning several decades inspired a discussion of women's changing roles through those decades. Members brought a favorite apron of their own or one inherited from a relative and shared their memories about the people who wore their aprons. If you know someone with an interesting collection,

Figure 3-4 "A Rose by Any Other Name" is a poster matching game of beautiful roses with literary names.

ask to borrow it or invite him or her to share it with the group. Display a small collection on the table or around the room if the items are larger. Think of creative topics that relate to the collection as well as interesting facts about the collection itself.

A perfect summer day is when the sun is shining, the breeze is blowing, the birds are singing, and the lawn mower is broken.

—James Dent

Summertime fun, past and present, is a just-for-fun June topic. Begin the discussion by asking members "What was your favorite summer pastime as a child?" Compare their responses with how children spend their summers now, discussing the children who are spending time in the library this summer participating in the summer reading program. Give examples of program activities, current favorite books and materials and summer reading statistics. Gather timeless games such as jacks and a ball, a hula-hoop, a jump rope, and pick up sticks to decorate the center of the table and display books with titles that reflect light summertime reading for browsing and check out. Small bagels with cream cheese and fruit are light summer refreshments.

AUGUST: TRAVEL

Ask a group member or a speaker who has recently returned from a trip to talk about his or her experiences and share souvenirs. A guest speaker who had returned from a trip to China had many interesting stories and items she brought back to the states. Display maps of the area, travel books on the country or state, and books by authors that live in that area for browsing and checkout. Allow time for questions and discussion from the group and serve a treat or refreshment that reflects the culture of the trip destination. Fortune cookies were fun for the China discussion.

For another approach to the travel discussion, ask the group to share their personal travel experiences and favorite vacations. It is amazing how many different modes of transportation and vast horizons one small group of people has experienced. Display books and videos on travel and vacation planning or novels set in different countries and pass out bookmarks listing cheap travel sites on the Internet.

SEPTEMBER: CELEBRATE YOUR FREEDOM TO READ

"Only the suppressed word is dangerous."

—Ludwig Börne

Explain Banned Books Week to the group and review a selection of challenged books using the "Pass It On" game described for January. Lead the members to comment on why they think the books were challenged, then share the real reasons. Hand out a copy of The First Amendment and a list of the most frequently challenged books of the year. Display videos of movies depicting censorship for checkout: *Storm Center*, *Fahrenheit 451, 1984, The Seven Minutes*, and *Inherit the Wind*. Make or purchase bookmarks with the phrase "Celebrate Your Freedom to Read" and the date of Banned Books Week, hand out word search puzzles of challenged book titles, and serve coffee cake and sliced apples with caramel dip.

OCTOBER: TEEN READ WEEK/KITCHEN GADGETS

Share "Teen Read Week" with the seniors in the Coffee Club by inviting the Young Adult (YA) Librarian to the meeting to talk about YA books and other materials and programs. Spark an interesting and lively discussion by showing photos of teens participating in programs and talking about books the guests may have read as teens. Ask the YA Librarian to talk about some of the new popular YA books, and encourage group members to check out some of the new YA titles and reread some of their old favorites. Allow time for questions and discussion. This is a good way to introduce the group to other staff members and keep them informed about what other departments and age groups are doing at the library.

"Handy Dandy Kitchen Gadgets" is a show and tell program that asks members to bring their favorite old kitchen gadgets. Borrow more gadgets for the program from co-workers and friends. Everyone guesses what the gadgets are and the owner can add any history or trivia about his or her own gadget that makes it a favorite. Display books on collectible kitchen utensils and culinary mystery novels and serve pumpkin bread and small pretzels as fall refreshments.

NOVEMBER: NATIVE AMERICAN MONTH/NATIONAL CHILDREN'S BOOK WEEK

Research the Native Americans who lived in your area and share historical facts and local legends. Explain why Native American Indians

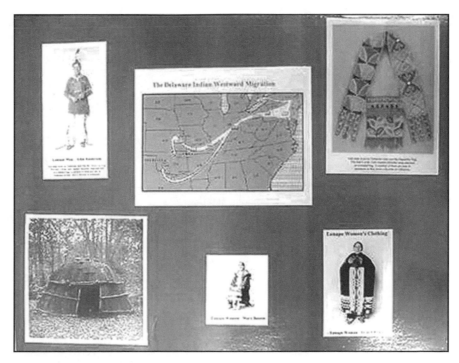

Figure 3-5 Pictures of famous Native Americans, homes, tools, and artifacts add visual interest to the discussion.

Month is celebrated. Start the discussion by asking if any members of the group have Native American heritage and ask the group to bring artifacts they may have or ask a local collector to come and share an arrowhead or stone tool collection. Print Native American words on poster cards and show the pronunciation and meaning of the native language, or learn some Indian sign language and demonstrate. Print Native American recipes to hand out and serve corn meal muffins and trail mix as refreshments.

A house without books is like a room without windows. No man has a right to bring up children without surrounding them with books.... Children learn to read being in the presence *of books*.

—Heinrich Mann

Figure 3-6 Coffee Club discussions about holidays are a great time to share and learn with our multicultural neighbors.	
December January February	Hanukkah, Kwanzaa, Santa Lucia Day, TET Nguyen-Dan, Xin Nian and Deng Jie, Tu Bi-Shevat, Eid-Al-Adha, Advent, Christmas, New Year's Day, Martin Luther King, Jr. Day, President's Day
March April May	Mardi Gras, Lent, Easter, Purim, Passover, Qing Ming, Holi, Hina Masuri, St. Joseph's Day, April Fool's Day, Hana Matsuri, Earth Day, Arbor Day, May Day, Cinco de Mayo, Tango-no-sekku, Kodomono-Hi, Mother's Day, Memorial Day
June July August	Shavnot, Obon Festival, Duanwu Jie, Father's Day, Flag Day, Juneteenth, Independence Day, Tanabata, Bastille Day, Mormon Pioneer Day, Hiroshima Day, Assumption Day, Women's Equality Day
September October November	Diwali, Rosh Hashanah, Ramadan, Id-Ul-Fitr, Zhongqiu Jie, Yom Kippur, Chongyang Jie, Labor Day, Columbus Day, Halloween, Veteran's Day, Thanksgiving Day, Mexican Independence Day, Itse Selu, United Nations Day, All Saints' Day, Dia de los Muertos

National Children's Book Week is another opportunity for the members of the group to become acquainted with library staff from other departments. Invite the Children's Librarian to talk to the group about story times, special current and upcoming programs, and children's book awards. Display Caldecott and Newbery Award books and ask the Children's Librarian to read from a few and show the artwork. Many of these books appeal to all ages, and Appendix E lists children's chapter and picture books that appeal to seniors. Leave time for questions and discussion with the librarian and serve doughnuts and mixed nuts.

DECEMBER: HOLIDAY TRADITIONS

Christmas is the season for kindling the fire of hospitality in the hall, the genial flame of charity in the heart.

—Washington Irving

Ask members to share their favorite holiday traditions and plan some fun activities for the holiday meeting. Read *The Right Family Christmas* (see resources) aloud while the group members play a gift game, passing gifts to the left or right. Play Christmas Bingo and use peppermints for the markers, share Christmas trivia, or make a trivia quiz game. Hold a "White Elephant" gift exchange in which guests bring a strange, playful, or tacky "gag" gift to exchange. A coffee mug with packages of cappuccino or tea and a holiday bookmark is a nice gift to give each member. Serve stollen, party mix, and mints.

Discussions featuring Hanukkah or Kwanzaa traditions can follow the same format. After giving some historical background, encourage members to share their family traditions, serve traditional refreshments, and play traditional games. Holidays throughout the year can be topics for discussion.

RESOURCES

FOR BOOK DISCUSSION:

1. Jacobsohn, Rachel, W. 1994. *The Reading Group Handbook.* New York: Hyperion.
2. Paz, Donna, and Mark Kaufman, eds. 2002. *Reading Group Choices: Selections for Lively Book Discussions.* Nashville: Paz and Associates.
3. Slezak, Ellen, ed. 2000. *The Book Group Book.* Chicago: Chicago Review Press.

4. Park Ridge Public Library. "Book Discussion Guides." www.park-ridge.il.us/library/bkdiscguide.html.

5. Promotion, Inc. "BookPage Online." www.bookpage.com.

6. Vintage Reading Group Center. "Tips: Ideas for Discussion." www.randomhouse.com/vintage/read/tips.html.

FOR FILM DISCUSSION:

1. MPLC: Motion Picture Licensing Corporation. www.mplc.com/index2.htm.

2. Movie Licensing USA. "Public Libraries." www.movlic.com/library.html.

FOR COFFEE CLUB: FRUGAL LIVING:

1. Dacyczyn, Amy. 1998. *Complete Tightwad Gazette: Promoting Thrift As A Viable Alternative Lifestyle.* New York: Villard.

2. Hunt, Mary, ed. "Cheapskate Monthly." www.cheapskate monthly.com.

FOR COFFEE CLUB: ST. VALENTINES DAY

1. Brown, Fern G. 1983. *Valentine's Day.* New York: F. Watts.

2. Kalman, Bobbie. 1986. *We Celebrate Valentine's Day.* Toronto, New York: Crabtree.

3. Tobori, Lena, and Nathasha Tabori Fried, eds. 2000. *The Little Big Book of Love.* New York: William Morrow.

4. Annie's Home Page. "Annie's Valentine History Page." www.annieshomepage.com/valhistory.html.

5. History Channel. "History of Valentine's Day." www.history channel.com/exhibits/valentine.

6. *Valentine's Day Actiphile.* Madison, Wisconsin: BiFolkal Productions.

FOR COFFEE CLUB: BLACK HISTORY MONTH

1. Haney, Elissa. "The History of Black History." www.info please.com/spot/bhmintro1.html.

FOR COFFEE CLUB: ST. PATRICK'S DAY

1. Gibbons, Gail. 1994. *St. Patrick's Day.* New York: Holiday

House.

2. *St. Patrick's Day Actiphile*. Madison, Wisconsin: BiFolkal Productions.

FOR COFFEE CLUB: ROSES

1. Martin, Clair G. 1997. *100 English Roses for the American Garden*. New York: Workman.
2. Sheen, Joanna. 1995. *Fragrance and Flower Craft*. London: Salamander
3. "Rose Trivia." www.aboutflowers.com/holidays_b5d.html.
4. Floramex. "How to Make Rose Potpourri." www.floramex.com/lirosepot.htm.
5. Woman's Heart. "Beauty Tips." www.womanht.com/beauty/rosewater.htm.

FOR COFFEE CLUB: APRONS:

1. Cheney, Joyce. 2000. *Aprons: Icons of the American Home*. Philadelphia: Running Press.
2. "Sweet Memories Are Tied in Apron Strings." *Reminisce* 9, no. 3 (May/June 1999): 32-33.
3. Margie's Place. "My Ode to Grandma's Apron." http://patsy-rose224.tripod.com/apron.html.

FOR COFFEE CLUB: BANNED BOOKS:

1. "First Amendment to the Bill of Rights." Chicago: American Library Association. www.ala.org/Content/NavigationMenu/Our_Association/Offices/Intellectual_Freedom3/First_Amendment/First_Amendment.htm.
2. "Banned Books Week." Chicago: American Library Association. www.ala.org/Content/NavigationMenu/Our_Association/Offices/Intellectual_Freedom3/Banned_Books_Week/Banned_Books_Week.htm

FOR COFFEE CLUB: KITCHEN GADGETS:

1. Celchar, Jane H. 1982. *Kitchen and Gadgets—1920-1950*. Wallace-Homestead.
2. Kalman, Bobbie. 1990. *The Kitchen*. Toronto: Crabtree.
3. Lindenberger, Jan. 1996. *Fun Kitchen Collectibles*. Atglen, PA: Schiffer.

FOR COFFEE CLUB: NATIVE AMERICAN MONTH

1. Bush, George W. "National American Indian Heritage Month Proclamation" www.defenselink.mil/specials/nativeamerican01/proclamation.html

2. "Recipe Source: Native American Recipes" www.recipesource.com/ethnic/americas/native.

FOR COFFEE CLUB: HOLIDAY TRADITIONS:

1. JT Software. "Bingomaker." www.jtsoftware.com/bingomaker.html.

2. Family Games. "Christmas Trivia Game." http://familygames.com/features/quizzes/xmasquiz.html.

3. Pow Wow Online. "The Right Family Christmas." http://members.tripod.com/CubBobwhite/skits/skit37.htm.

4 OFFER INFORMATIVE AND ENTERTAINING PROGRAMS AT THE LIBRARY

A library should be like a pair of open arms.

—Roger Rosenblatt

OVERVIEW

Because senior adults have a wide variety of interests, the most satisfactory approach to bringing them into the library is to provide a good quality program for a smaller target audience rather than to create a general program for a larger audience. The Never Too Late Group of Boston Public Library is the oldest library-sponsored program in the country for adults age sixty and over. Established in 1950, the group meets for informal educational programs including lectures, films, videos, and concerts on Thursday afternoons October through June.

This chapter is a collection of scheduled programs and ideas for special occasions that we have used successfully in our library and that other libraries across the country have graciously shared. Many of the programs can be done by the library staff, others use guest speakers found in your own communities. Ask the Friends group to serve light refreshments after the programs to give the audience opportunity to socialize. It's "Never Too Late" to start programming for your senior audience!

SUMMER AND WINTER READING PROGRAMS

A summer or winter reading program will encourage reading and participation by adding a bit of fun with prize incentives. The patron fills out a book rating form for each item read or records time spent reading to enter a weekly drawing or end of program drawing for a grand prize. Create different book rating forms and prizes with a theme for each year's program by either adapting the state library's reading theme or making one just for the senior audience. The two following programs provide different approaches to creating reading incentives. The first gives everyone an opportunity to win a prize regardless of the amount of reading accomplished, and the second sets goals and provides awards for those who finish the program.

NEVER JUDGE A BOOK BY ITS MOVIE

Never judge a book by its movie.

—J. W. Eagan

Try this program through the winter when seniors have more time to read a book, see the movie, and compare the two. Create the form illustrated in figure 4-1 for participants to enter a weekly prize drawing and also hold a grand prize drawing to end the program. Local merchants are good sources for prize donations; try a local restaurant or movie theatre for gift certificates. The title of the program lends itself well to a display of books made into movies with the videos of the movies, promoting both collections, and you can follow the program with a display of the favorite titles in both formats to attract more readers and movie watchers.

Figure 4-1 Patrons can vote for the book or the movie and enter weekly drawings with one form.

Never Judge a Book By Its Movie!!

Title _____

Check one:
_____ I liked the book better!
_____ I liked the movie better!

Name _____

Phone _____

TEA-RRIFIC READS

You can't get a cup of tea big enough or a book long enough to suit me.

—C.S. Lewis

Build a program around a theme that will appeal to seniors. For example, "Tea-rrific Reads" uses tea bags and tea gift baskets as incentives. Create a brochure that includes the program description and a bookmark to cut off for recording the reading hours necessary to complete the program. Two tea bags in a small gift box made with an Accu-cut die is an inexpensive prize to award everyone who completes the program, and the bookmarks with the recorded reading hours are returned for entries in the grand prize drawings for gift baskets, which can include a mug, assorted teas, and tea biscuits. A fun social closing for the program is a tea party for the participants, described later in this chapter.

COOKING PROGRAMS

Cooking is at once child's play and adult joy.
And, cooking done with care is an act of love.

—Craig Clairborne

COOKING FOR ONE OR TWO

Invite a nutritionist from the County Extension Office, hospital, or grocery to speak about cooking healthy meals for one or two people. After a lifetime of cooking for a family, it can be difficult to know how to cook meals for one or two people without having a lot of leftovers. Seniors are also often advised to change their diets to eat healthier, so they sometimes feel they are learning to cook all over again. Suggested topics for the speaker to address are how to shop for two, store food, and trim fat, cholesterol, sugar, and salt from favorite recipes. Invite the participants to exchange favorite recipes. If the nutritionist is doing a cooking demonstration, be sure to have adequate electrical connections and table space and ask the nutritionist to bring any needed equipment. Providing pre-registration for the program or limiting the number of guests will aid in planning if food is being sampled. Provide paper goods for serving samples.

CHOCOLATE PROGRAMS

Other things are just food. But chocolate's chocolate.

—Patrick Skene Catling

Invite a local chef, baker or candy maker to do a demonstration on making chocolates. You can offer a hands-on workshop if you have a friend or relative who is willing to share his or her knowledge about making molded chocolates. Invite the public to bake favorite chocolate creations and hold a Chocolate Bake Off with local celebrities as judges and create a booklet of the recipes used. Solicit Hershey's and local chocolate candy companies for free donations for door prizes, and present a chocolate cookbook to the Bake Off winner. February is a good time for the chocolate program to connect with a Valentine's Day theme. Display cooking-with-chocolate books and romance books!

COOKING PROGRAMS WITH OLDER ADULTS

Homemade bread, butter, popcorn, tea, and snow are the main course ingredients served up in *Stirring Up Memories: Food Programs with Older Adults.* (Check the resource list for more information about this book.) Several reproducible recipes in large print, tips for presenting cooking programs, and variations for adapting with audiences with different abilities and limitations make this book a helpful guide for conducting cooking programs with the older crowd. Cooperative projects are described in detail for use with Alzheimer patients, and interesting bits of history and trivia are included to share with the participants.

CRAFT PROGRAMS

Invite a local crafts person to demonstrate his or her craft and lead a group in making their own creations. If you have expertise in a craft, share your knowledge with a class of seniors. Depending on the complexity of the project you choose, the craft program can stand alone, or a discussion can be held while working. A seating arrangement of four tables pushed together will allow a small group of a dozen participants to access craft materials, see the demonstration, and talk to each other. Your budget will go farther if you collect craft materials from your family and co-workers. Seniors may learn a new craft they can continue enjoying at home or create a gift for a loved one. Some ideas for craft programs are:

- Lead a guided discussion on managing holiday stress while creating holiday decorations. Choose a simple project from craft books or magazines. Martha Stewart's books, magazines, Web site, and television show are good sources for quick holiday craft ideas.

- Conduct a whole series of holiday craft sessions, completing a different craft each week or one complex craft. Some suggestions from *Elder-Berries* for a craft series are: padded picture frames, bread dough ornaments, cathedral window pincushions, and molded chocolates.

- Invite a local scrapbooking artist to come a lead a creative session covering the basics and completing a page or two of a scrapbook. Ask participants to bring a few photographs for their pages.

- Create greeting cards with rubber stamps, inks, and embossing powders.

- Invite a potter to demonstrate his or her work and guide the group in creating simple clay projects such as a slab pot.

- Paint clay flower pots with stenciling, sponging, tole painting or other interesting techniques. Display a painted pot with garden items in it (garden gloves, a trowel and seed packets) to show what a nice gift it will make.

- Print out a year calendar made on a computer, leaving space at the top for a photo. Glue on the photo and frame with fancy papers or stamps, laminate and attach magnet strips on the back for the refrigerator.

HOBBY PROGRAMS

Hobbies are not only interesting pastimes; often they can save money and sometimes make money! Seniors tend to become experts in their hobbies because they usually have more time to devote to them. Invite the senior experts to lead these programs and ask them to show some tips and tricks that make their favorite hobbies easier, more satisfying and productive.

WINDOW BOX AND CONTAINER GARDENING

One of the most delightful things about a garden is the anticipation it provides.

—W.E. Johns

Window box gardens are easy to install, simple to plant, fun to care for, and ideal for sunny spots on patios and balconies. Plan this program with a senior who loves to garden and likes to talk about it. A window box or container, soil, sand or gravel, peat moss, trowel, plants, water, and gloves are needed to demonstrate a planting. Consider the site, weather, and sun time when choosing plants. Space plants eight inches apart, planting taller plants in the back, lower ones in front of the container. Ask the senior expert to give tips on watering and fertilizing. This program would be nice to hold outside in a courtyard, on a deck or patio. Display gardening books and videos. Give the finished planted container a special spot at the library so the program attendees can monitor its progress through the growing season.

GARDENING FOR SENIORS

Invite a Master Gardener to speak about the medicinal and psychological benefits of gardening, and ask him or her to share tips on garden design that will make gardening easier, including raised beds, trellis gardening, and container gardening. The speaker can also demonstrate tools that make tending gardens easier. Check the resource list in this chapter for the Master Gardener Web site, and also check if the county extension agent or local garden centers may have speakers for your programs. Programs about growing specific favorites such as iris or roses will also interest seniors.

HERBS 101

When in doubt, use thyme.

—Grass Roots Herb Society

Invite an herbalist to speak about herbs. Growing tips, recipes, historical and contemporary uses, and drying instructions are some of the topics to cover. The herbalist may bring potted herbs, otherwise borrow some from gardener friends or bring a variety of cut sprigs of herbs from the grocery. Display herbal remedies books, herb cookbooks, and herb gardening books.

FLOWER ARRANGING

Invite a member of a local garden club, a florist or a hobby store teacher to come and demonstrate floral arrangement. Ask them to talk about where to buy fresh and silk flowers, how to select colors, and how to create designs. A fun flower quiz that shows what your favorite arrangement style is available at www.aboutflowers.com/giftideas-quiz.html. Ask for flower donations from garden clubs and florists and add "Bring a vase!" to the publicity for the program to turn this program into a workshop. Display books and videos on floral design, flower arranging, and decorating with flowers.

BIRD WATCHING

**I value my garden more for being full of blackbirds
    than of cherries,
and very frankly give them fruit for their songs.**

—Joseph Addison

Check www.audubon.org for Audubon centers near you and ask a speaker to talk about the birds in your area. Show digital slides or a PowerPoint program of area birds, share tips on attracting birds to your backyard, play bird calls on tape or CD, tell how to provide shelter and food for birds in winter, and hand out bird seed and suet treat recipes and bird name checklists for beginning bird watchers. The county extension office may also have a speaker list and materials for handouts for this program. There are many beautiful bird books to display for browsing; check your library's collection.

ANTIQUES AND COLLECTIBLES

Senior patrons may rediscover a keepsake and wonder what its value is today, so invite an antique dealer or museum representative to speak about antiques and collectibles. New collectors want to know what features to look for, what the marks and signatures mean, and how to spot fakes for favorite collectibles such as dolls, postcards, books, coins, stamps, records, glass, and ceramics. Ask the dealer to discuss how antiques are valued and what makes something collectible. A knowledgeable speaker can share a bit of history while talking about the items.

Hold an "Antiques Road Show @ the Library" and invite patrons to bring a favorite item to be identified and valued by area antique specialists. Each specialist should have a table and chair as this can be a long program. Combine this idea with a Collector's Fair and invite local collectors to display their collectibles. This won't be a buying and selling event, but dealers can make contacts and it will be very informative for the participants. Serve beverages, create a bibliography of books and Web sites for collectors, and have book displays for browsing while waiting.

GAME PROGRAMS

Scrabble Tournaments are easy and inexpensive programs, and players can bring their own games when they register. Set up card tables or game tables for four players each or divide players evenly. Go over the game rules, explain challenges, and show the dictionary the referee will use for making decisions. Each player records his own points on a separate score sheet and dictionaries are not allowed to be used by the players while composing words. The first round is forty minutes long and players are given a three minute warning to complete the last round of turns. Serve refreshments during the break while the scores are tallied by the referees. For a "King of the Hill" tournament, the players are sorted by their scores for the second round; the four with the highest scores play together, the next highest four play together, and so on. The second round of play lasts for thirty minutes and players are once again given a three minute warning to complete a round. The scores are tallied and the total points from the first round and second round are added together. The one player with the highest total for both games is the "King of the Hill." Award a small prize like a Scrabble dictionary to the King. Checkers, Chinese checkers, and chess are more tournament games to try with seniors.

HISTORY PROGRAMS

LOCAL HISTORY

Public libraries have a treasure chest of interesting photographs in their local history collections that can be shared in a digital slide show or PowerPoint program. Scan images, add a caption or title to each one, and plan a themed presentation with time for discussion, questions and personal stories. Themes to consider are old barns, covered bridges, or one room schools from the local area. Invite members of the Historical Society to come and take notes, and invite students who are working on independent history projects.

You can also focus on local historical events and characters and invite a speaker who does character portrayals. For example, Douglas Bahnsen of Ohio (call 419-874-9860 to schedule) offers "Ohio History–A Journey into Ohio's Amazing Past," a series of five programs portraying an early settler, Johnny Appleseed, a canal boat captain, John Muir, and Henry David Thoreau. Write or call your state or regional library to ask for a list of speakers in your area who do character portrayals.

Contact nearby colleges for speakers from the anthropology or archeology department, the local museum, or a nearby Indian Reservation who can talk about Native Americans who lived in your area. Local legends, artifacts, language, homes, games, and arts and crafts are a few of the topics that would be interesting not only to seniors, but to all ages.

DECADE PROGRAMS

Explore the fascinating "Roaring Twenties" with a slide show from the "Remembering 1924" Bi-Folkal kit, and/or *Flapper Story,* a twenty-nine minute film. Ask local collectors and antique dealers to show and tell about some of their treasures from the '20s. Share interesting bits of history from books about the 1920s and display these and other library materials for browsing and checkout.

Show the PBS video series on the Great Depression, *Coping with the Depression,* and invite the audience to share their memories. How did their families cope? What do they remember eating? What games did they play as children?

A "Fabulous Fifties" program will attract older Baby Boomers. There are many possibilities for topics and displays including '50s décor, cars, music, headlines, toys, TV, comics, and fashion. Invite a DJ from an oldies station, use the Bi-Folkal "Fabulous Fifties" kit with slides, or talk about the book *Remembering Woolworths: A Nostalgic Look at the World's Most Favorite Five and Dime.* This program can be a whole evening of displays of '50s memorabilia and music. You can have a sock hop, a James Dean/Sandra Dee look-alike contest, and serve ice cream sodas!

WAR PROGRAMS

Honor local veterans, educate the community, and commemorate our country's wars with programs held around Memorial Day, Independence Day, Veteran's Day, or Pearl Harbor Day. Several program ideas are offered in *Serving Seniors: a Resource Manual for Missouri Libraries*, including "World War II–Life on the Homefront" and "The 38th Parallel, Remembering the Korean War." Invite veterans, war history buffs, and war memorabilia collectors to come and share their memories, knowledge, and collections. The local historical society is a good resource for speakers and other resources, and the local museum might have collections you can borrow for a display. Hold a "Salute to the USO Canteens" open house program in the community room, invite seniors to bring in World War II memorabilia like uniforms, letters, mess kits, and ration books for display, invite a band to play '40s music, and decorate in red, white, and blue.

MORE HISTORY PROGRAM IDEAS

- Present "This Road Runs Through It," a program about famous historical routes through your state like the National Road and Route 66. Show photo slides of the road building project and famous roadside stops and collect tourist information for planning a trip along the route.

- For a "Fireside Chat" series, focus on a different famous, interesting person for each program. Display books, movies, and memorabilia and talk about their lives. Suggestions for subjects are: Grandma Moses, the Delaney Sisters, Jim Henson, Pocahontas, Erma Bombeck, Dave Thomas, Bob Hope, Johnny Appleseed, Will Rogers, Betty White, Art Linkletter, Maya Angelou, Buffalo Bill Cody, Irving Berlin, Laura Ingalls Wilder, Roy Rogers, and Dale Evans.

- Contact area teams for local sports heroes who can serve as speakers. Generate discussion with an eye-catching display including library materials about the team and the sport, biographies of the players, a uniform, sports equipment, and team memorabilia. Talk about past sports heroes from the local area.

- Celebrate statewide anniversaries with "100 Years of Flight" or bicentennial celebrations. Plan character portrayal programs, make displays, and hold photo slide shows featuring the historical people, sites, and events of your state or province.

- Contact local museums about their Museum-to-Go collections that can travel to off-site locations for displays and programs.

- Show historical films such as *Riding the Rails*, a film about teens hopping freight cars during the Depression. These film programs are a great time for seniors to meet old and new friends, and the library staff can promote the collection and services.

GENEALOGY

Give beginning genealogists a head start with this informative program. Invite the local history librarian or a speaker from the historical or genealogical society to help the audience make a plan to search public and family records for their family's history. This could be a series of programs covering where to begin research, what to look for, what questions to ask, how to identify good leads, and how to organize material and document resources. If the audience size is limited, this program can be held in the local history room, and participants can have hands-on experience. Family record forms are perfect handouts.

PERFORMANCE AND ENTERTAINMENT PROGRAMS

With the addition of performance and entertainment programs, the public library can become the cultural center of the community. The library can provide the room, schedule the performers, and publicize the event; the performers do the rest. Our contributors have had success with these programs:

- Show movies on Friday afternoons and serve light refreshments afterwards. Seniors can visit with each other and discuss the movie.
- Invite seniors to celebrate at "Ring in the New Year," held in the afternoon on the Friday before New Year's Eve. Decorate the community room cabaret style, hire a live band, and serve sparkling cider in champagne glasses with other light refreshments.
- Invite ethnic folk dance groups to perform in costume or feature a series of ethnic folk music performances.
- Host a dance to celebrate Senior Citizens Month

with refreshments and live entertainment featuring the big band music of Glenn Miller, Benny Goodman, Artie Shaw, Woody Herman, Tommy and Jimmy Dorsey, Duke Ellington, Henry James, Patti Page, Ella Fitzgerald, and Frank Sinatra. A dance instructor can teach swing dance steps.

- Host a "Senior Showcase" for seniors who can sing, dance, recite poetry, or lead in a sing-along. The library staff or Friends volunteers can book the program, set up the room, introduce performers, and provide coffee and cookies.

- Host a music series featuring a different type of music—barber shop quartet, gospel choir, madrigal singers, or a trio—at each program. Contact musical friends to perform. Musicians will bring their own instruments, but a tuned piano should be available. Provide programs that tell about the performer and the music, introduce the performers, and display sheet music, instructional books, and music collections.

- Present an informational program about a music style, interspersing, for example, a history of Barbershop Quartets and Sweet Adelines with recorded music and photo slides.

TRAVEL PROGRAMS

I travel not to go anywhere, but to go.
I travel for travel's sake.
The great affair is to move.

—Robert Louis Stevenson

Almost everyone dreams of traveling when they retire, and travel programs give seniors a chance to share their travel experiences with interested audiences. The audiences are not only entertained and enlightened by these programs, but also learn sound travel tips and hear of places they may want to visit. Seniors who are unable to travel also like to hear about far away places. Display books relating to the featured destination, decorate the room with maps and a globe, and provide door prizes and refreshments reflecting the culture.

Try the travel professionals for informative speakers: travel agents, the Chamber of Commerce, the Department of Conservation, the Department of Natural Resources, AAA, AARP, and Elderhostel. Travel agents can talk about the most popular destinations and tours, an Elderhostel ambassador can introduce seniors to travel opportunities with their peers, and others can focus on one-day trips and nearby his-

Figure 4-2 Invite local travelers to talk about their adventures.

Tuesday Travelogues

Travelogues are scheduled for the 4th Tuesday
of each month at 1 p.m.

Registration is not required.
August 27 Eastern Europe - Ed Feathers
September 24 Kilimanjaro – Rich and Sue Freeman
October 22 Brazil – Charles Carlton
November 26 Northern Italy – Harry Hart

Fairport Public Library
1 Village Landing
Fairport, NY 14450
http://fairportlibrary.org

Hours
Monday – Thursday 10 – 9
Friday 10 – 6
Saturday 9 – 5
Sunday 2 – 5
(October 1 – April 30)

torical sites. Collect packets of information from nearby tourist areas and the state tourism agency for handouts and make a flyer with Web sites for discount travel.

Travelogues held in the afternoon are popular weekly or monthly programs through fall, winter, and spring. Invite area residents to share their travel experiences through a slide show, souvenirs, and books and offer to provide a projector and screen for the room. Word of mouth about these programs and networking with other libraries will keep you supplied with audiences and presenters.

Special guests who have traveled to faraway exotic places are excellent presenters. John Gardner has been a popular speaker at our own library, where he has spoken of his travels to Antarctica and Tristan da Cunha. Recent trips to St. Helena and Easter Island promise to be topics of future programs. A book display with program information publicizes the event, although his name now attracts the audience. One of our seniors enjoyed the Antarctica program so much she took a trip there!

SENIOR TEAS

There are few hours in life more agreeable than the hour dedicated to the ceremony known as afternoon tea.

—Henry James

This program is as enjoyable to prepare as it is to attend. Host a tea as a finale to a reading program or as a special event anytime. Require pre-registration, and if a specific group will be invited, send invitations early and ask for reservations. With a little imagination, you can transform your meeting room or community room into a tea room using card tables or square tables covered with borrowed tablecloths or paper covers, teapots borrowed from coworkers, friends, or a collector, and flowers as lovely centerpieces. Set the tables with pretty coordinated paper plates, cups, and napkins and play soft music as the guests arrive. Favors and bookmarks are extra touches to add to the tables and nametags help guests get to know each other.

A short program presented by library staff or a guest speaker before the tea provides a theme and generates conversation. Have the hostesses take time to visit with the guests in keeping with the spirit of an afternoon tea. Provide a variety of teas, hold a door prize drawing for a book bag, a mug with a variety of tea bags, or a miniature tea set, and display books about the program theme for browsing and checkout. Friends of the Library groups and donations from local businesses can

Figure 4-3 Request an RSVP to your Tea Party invitations so you can plan seating and refreshments.

An Invitation to Tea

When: Wednesday, May 15, 2002
2:00-4:00 p.m.

Where: Coshocton Public Library

What: Please join us for a program on making soaps and lotions presented by Lori Burton. Enjoy refreshments provided by the Friends of the Library.

Who: Residents of Coshocton County nursing homes

RSVP: Please call the Coshocton Public Library by Wednesday, May 8 with an approximate number of residents who will attend.

help fund this program. If there is no charge for the presentation, be sure to present the guest speaker with a thank you note and a small gift of appreciation. Try one of the following tea party themes:

- Invite an herbalist to talk about herbs and herbal teas. Wrap herbal tea bags with tulle and tie with a ribbon for favors and place a bookmark with a tea quote at each place setting. Display potted herb plants and herbal teas and serve small muffins and cookies, cream cheese sandwiches, and tea.

- Invite a doll collector to display and talk about his or her dolls and how he or she began collecting. Special, foreign, and old dolls are especially interesting to see and hear about. Distribute ceramic teaspoons with a ribbon tied on the handle as favors and serve cream cheese sandwiches, fancy cookies, mints, and fresh strawberries served in small muffin papers.

- Invite a soap maker to provide a brief history of the changes in soap making, explain how soaps and lotions are made, and discuss the present day luxury of pampering oneself with scented bath salts and lotions. Small scented soaps wrapped in tulle and ribbons to coordinate with the table settings make pretty favors. Serve cream cheese sandwiches, party cookies, and fruit cups.

- Invite the owner of a tearoom to present a program on the Traditional Afternoon Tea, the history of an afternoon tea, and the proper way to serve it. Display a traditional tea setting, serve cucumber sandwiches, fresh fruit, thumbprint cookies, and mints, and provide small picture frames as favors.

- Present a "First Ladies Tea," choosing a few of the most memorable First Ladies as a focus, and begin the program with readings and discussion about the role of the First Lady. Check the resources list for readings about Abigail Adams, Dolley Madison, Frances Cleveland, Edith Roosevelt and Eleanor Roosevelt. Decorate in red, white, and blue. Make an inexpensive, attractive centerpiece for each table by filling quart canning jars with sand and inserting red, white, or blue votive candles. Tie red and blue star garland around the top and place the jars on top of red, white and blue cardboard stars and scatter confetti (stars and U.S. flags) around the jars on white plastic table covers. Make bookmarks for everyone with this quote from Eleanor Roosevelt: "Women are like teabags. They don't know how strong they are until they get into hot water."

I dreamed of a wedding of elaborate elegance,
A church filled with family and friends.
I asked him what kind of a wedding he wished for,
He said one that would make me his wife.

—Author Unknown

- Present a tea with the theme "Wedding Legends and Traditions." Share the origins of popular wedding traditions and ask guests to share their memories about their own wedding and interesting weddings they have attended. Compare old traditions with new contemporary weddings and talk about celebrity

Figure 4-4 Turn your meeting room into a tea room with card tables and pretty table settings.

weddings, royal weddings, and unconventional weddings. Bring wedding dresses or veils for show-and-tell and serve white cake, mints, and nuts.

LOCAL MEDIA GUEST SPEAKERS

Seniors read the papers, listen to the radio and watch local news and weather on television every day. The people that bring us the news and weather are so familiar, they have a somewhat celebrity status and make great guest speakers for library programs.

- Invite a local news anchor to explain how the news is put on the air, talk about interesting news stories, and explain how one becomes a news anchor.
- Invite a local meteorologist to discuss local weather issues and records, weather safety, different types of clouds, forecasting, and weather folklore.
- Invite a radio talk show host or DJ to talk about

interesting guests, discuss how the show is put together, and offer behind-the-scenes trade secrets.

- Invite a local newspaper reporter and a photographer to talk about how they hear about news stories, who decides what gets into the paper, how newspapers are published, and what goes into a good news story.

WRITING PROGRAMS

MEMOIR WRITING WORKSHOPS

There are thousands of thoughts lying within a man that he does not know till he takes up the pen and writes.

—William Makepeace Thackeray

Preserving personal history by writing memoirs, preserving letters and photos, and recording oral histories on video and audio will enrich the lives of the writers and of those who will read their writings in the future. The stories can help us understand the older people in our lives

Figure 4-5 Teach the art of making books by hand and your workshop audience will have beautiful unique journals for writing their memoirs.

and help us understand who we are and where we came from. Writing memoirs is therapeutic for older adults, helping them find meaning and appreciation in their lives.

To attract an audience to the library for months, present a series of programs about how to preserve keepsakes, what to write, what to keep, and how to store memorabilia. The popular arts of bookmaking and scrapbooking will add an artistic and creative touch to the writing projects. A library writing group can choose to write biographies of local long time residents and local veterans and celebrities, individuals may want to learn how to record the memories of their oldest family members, and many seniors will want to write their memoirs for their children and grandchildren.

There are two different approaches to these programs: recording someone else's history or recording your own. Several resources are available to guide you in leading this workshop series yourself, if professionals or hobbyists are not available. The book *Musings, Memories, & Make Believe* has many questions in many categories that will work well for interviews or for handouts to give participants ideas for what to write in their own memoirs. *The Association of Personal Historians* Web site has a Coaching Corner with tips on the ways to capture memories and the Veteran's History Project at the Library of Congress Web site has a downloadable kit to guide you as well

Everyone has stories to tell! *You Can Write a Memoir* has suggestions for urging reticent writers to get started. For instance, ask your workshop audience to write about a specific event or time period such as a "first" event, a rite of passage, a coming-of-age experience, a memorable place, a vacation, or a holiday gathering, or suggest they bring a keepsake to a session to write about. Encourage painting a picture with words by using imagery and details and describing for all of the senses. Check the resource list for more information on all of these helpful guides.

"My Story" is an example of a three month summer series of workshops designed to encourage the preservation of personal histories by providing classes in bookmaking, painting, preservation of photos and letters, and presentation of memorabilia. A local historian can speak about the value of one's own history and the therapeutic benefit of expressing ones thoughts and memories and present a slide presentation of paintings by an artist who expressed his or her life experiences in paintings. Schedule each workshop to last one hour, provide any needed materials, and contact retirement and nursing homes so transportation can be arranged for any residents who would like to attend.

AUTHOR GUESTS

Local authors can inspire others to write. Invite a local author to lead a discussion on how to find a publisher, what publishers want, how to get published, and what experiences they have had in their quest to become a published author. The librarian can talk about the literary magazines, *Writers Market* books, and how-to-write books from the library collection.

If your library invites well-known authors to speak and sign books, keep in mind that afternoon sessions are more likely to attract a larger senior adult audience.

POETRY WORKSHOPS

Fun group projects at a poetry workshop can inspire the poet in all of us. You can find several ideas for exercises in the book *Exploring Our Lives: a Writing Handbook for Senior Adults.* Form poems such as a cinquain, haiku, or rhymed couplets are easy introductions to poetry writing.

WRITING GROUPS

Start a writing group if your library doesn't already host one. Besides memoirs and poetry, writers can work on diaries, dream journals, short stories, or children's picture books. Several writing project ideas can inspire new writers, and they will find confidence, develop a style, and find a voice with the input from an audience of fellow writers. Check the resources for interesting writing projects like writing a story from a photograph, and explore your library collection for books about writing exercises to help your group develop their skills.

RESOURCES

FOR OVERVIEW

1. Boston Public Library. "Services to Senior Adults." www.bpl.org/central/adult/senior.htm.

FOR CHOCOLATE:

1. Cheek, Jerrie S. "Welcome to My Chocolate Theme Page."

http://webtech.kennesaw.edu/jcheek3/chocolate.htm.

FOR COOKING:

1. Cole, Phyllis J. 1991. *Stirring Up Memories: Food Programs with Older Adults.* Madison, WI: Bi-Folkal Productions.

FOR POTTERY:

1. Hester, John. "Pottery Tutorial: Slab Construction." www.jhpottery.com/tutorial/slab.html.

FOR GARDENING:

1. Way, Joann. 1997. *Accessible Gardening: Tips and Techniques for Seniors and the Disabled.* Mechanicsburg, PA: Stackpole.
2. The American Horticultural Therapy Association. www.ahta.org.
3. Horticulture for All Homepage. http://ourworld.compuserve.com/homepages/Jane_Stoneham.
4. Mastergardener.com. http://mastergardeners.com.

FOR BIRD WATCHING:

1. Adams, George Martin. 2000. *Birdscaping Your Garden: A Practical Guide to Backyard Birds and the Plants that Attract Them.* Emmaus, PA: Rodale.
2. Roth, Sally. 2000. *Attracting Birds to Your Backyard. 536 Ways to Turn Your Yard and Garden into a Haven for Your Favorite Birds.* Emmaus, PA: Rodale.
3. National Audubon Society. "National Audubon Society Chapters: States." www.audubon.org/states.

FOR ANTIQUE COLLECTING:

1. Antiques USA. www.antiques-usa.com.
2. Kovels Online. www.tias.com/stores/kovels.

FOR DECADES PROGRAMS:

1. Boomerweb. "For the Baby Boomers Who Want to Go Back in Time." www.boomerweb.net.

2. Index Fifties Web. www.fiftiesweb.com.
3. Rewind the Fifties. www.loti.com.
4. Yesterdayland. http://humor.about.com/library/blds030299.htm

FOR GENEALOGY:

1. Allen, Desmond Walls. 1998. *First Steps in Genealogy: a Beginner's Guide to Researching Your Family History.* White Hall, VA: Betterway.
2. Croom, Emily Anne. 1995. *Unpuzzling Your Past: A Basic Guide to Genealogy.* White Hall, VA: Betterway.
3. Ancestry.com. www.ancestry.com/main.aspx.
4. Gengateway.com. www.gengateway.com.

FOR PERFORMANCE:

1. Harmonize.ws. "The Ultimate in Barbershop Links." www.harmonize.ws/links.
2. Sweet Adelines International. www.sweetadelineintl.org.

FOR FIRST LADIES:

1. Anthony, Carl Sferrazza. 2000. *America's First Families: an inside view of 200 years of private life in the White House.* New York: Simon and Schuster.
2. Anthony, Carl Sferrazza. 1991. *First Ladies: the saga of the presidents' wives and their power.* New York: W. Morrow.
3. Benet, Rosemary, and Stephen Vincent. 1933. *Book of Americans.* New York: Farrar and Rinehart.
4. Boller, Paul F. 1988 *Presidential Wives.* New York: Oxford University Press.
5. Caroli, Betty Boyd. 1987. *First Ladies.* New York: Oxford University Press.
6. Freedman, Russell. 1993. *Eleanor Roosevelt: a life of discovery.* New York: Clarion Books.
7. Hurd, Charles. 1966. *White House Story.* New York: Hawthorn Books.
8. McCullough, David. 2001. *John Adams.* New York: Simon and Schuster.
9. Means, Marianne. 1963. *Woman in the White House: the lives, times and influence of twelve notable first ladies.* New York: Random House.
10 Smith, Marie D., and Louise Durbin. 1966. *White House Brides.* Washington: Acropolis Books.

11 Whitcomb, John. 2000. *Real Life at the White House: two hundred years of daily life at America's most famous residence.* New York: Routledge.

FOR MEDIA GUEST SPEAKERS:

1. Ludlum, David McWilliams. 1997. *National Audubon Society Field Guide to North American Weather.* New York: Knopf.
2. Weather Affects, a Collection for Weather Enthusiasts. www.weatheraffects.com.
3. Wind and Weather. www.windandweather.com.

FOR WRITING:

1. Fox, Gabrielle. 2000. *Essential Guide to Making Handmade Books.* Cincinnati: North Light Books.
2. Hauser, Susan Carol. 2001. *You Can Write a Memoir.* Cincinnati: Writer's Digest Books.
3. Kazemek, Francis E. 2002. *Exploring Our Lives: a Writing Handbook for Senior Adults.* Santa Monica: Santa Monica Press.
4. Minor, Sandy. 1994. *Musings, Memories, & Make Believe.* Mt. Airy, MD: ElderSong Publications.
5. Tourtillott, Suzanne J.E. 2001. *Making and Keeping Creative Journals.* New York: Lark Books.
6. McDowell, Jeanne. 2002. "Book Smarts." *Time,* November 11: 80-81.
7. Rimer, Sara. 2002. "Turning to Autobiography for Emotional Growth in Old Age." *New York Times,* February 9, 2000. Reprinted in *Aging in America,* Olivia J. Smith, ed.
8. Stich, Sally S. 2002. "Stories to Keep." *Time,* November 11: bonus section.
9. Kansas City Public Library. "1000 Stories Project at Kansas City Public Library." www.kclibrary.org/sc/history/1000stories/contents.htm.
10. Association of Personal Historians. www.personal historians.org/
11. The Library of Congress. "Veteran's History Project." www.loc.gov/folklife/vets/kit.html

FOR ADDITIONAL PROGRAMMING RESOURCES:

1. Barrett, Shirley. 1980. *Parties With a Purpose: a Handbook for Activity Directors.* Springfield, IL: Charles Thomas.
2. Brennan, Jim. 1991. *Activities for the Mind: Memories,*

Dreams, and Thoughts Revisited. Bossier City, LA: Publicare Press.

3. Chase's Calendar of Events. 1994. Chicago: Contemporary Books.

4. Couch, Ernie and Jill, comp. 1992. *Ohio Trivia.* Nashville: Rutledge Hill Press.

5. Knoth, Marge. 1997. *Activity Planning at Your Fingertips.* Lafayette, IN: Valley Press.

6. Ohio Library Council. 1998. *Elderberries: Library Programs For Older Adults.* Columbus: Ohio Library Council.

7. Skarmeas, Nancy J., ed. 1991. *Remember When.* Nashville: Ideals Publishing Group.

8. *We Had Everything but Money.* 1992. Greendale, WI: Roy Reiman.

9. AARP. www.aarp.org.

10 D'Angelo, Barbara J. "21 Ideas for the 21st Century." American Library Association. www.ala.org/Content/NavigationMenu/RUSA/ Our_Association2/RUSA_Sections/MOUSS/Our_Section4/Committe es10/Library_Services_to_an_Aging_Population/Ideas_for_the_21st_ Century.htm

11. ElderSong Publications, Inc. www.eldersong.com.

12. Missouri State Library. *Serving Seniors: A Resource Manual for Missouri Libraries.* www.sos.mo.gov/library/development/services/ seniors/manual/default.asp.

5

PARTNER WITH OUTSIDE AGENCIES

**The nice thing about teamwork is that
you always have others on your side.**

—Margaret Carty

OVERVIEW

When libraries partner with other agencies, everyone benefits. Libraries need the support of senior voters and seniors need to know what services the library can offer them. High profile organizations such as AARP have large audiences of potential senior library patrons, and joint programs can help expand the library audience and increase the visibility of the partner in the community. These partner organizations need a neutral, reputable meeting place for their programs and a distribution place for their literature and the library can offer this service for free. Each agency can contribute its expertise to a program to share the workload, split the preparation time and expenses, and share publicity so more seniors will be informed.

May is National Senior Citizen's Month and Older Americans Month—a prime time to coordinate a first partnership. If some of the programs in this book seem like more than you can tackle alone, grab a partner! Explore your area for agencies that serve seniors and be creative when thinking of ways to collaborate with them. Successful partnerships produce interesting and beneficial programs that would not be possible without cooperation.

Begin with a plan to find out what your community has to offer. We describe specific partnerships and programs to give you an idea of the possibilities and show how the partners work together. The chapter ends with a list of possible partners and contacts to expand your senior audience.

Figure 5-1 The calendar offers several perfect occasions for partnering with outside agencies.	
January	Senior Women's Travel Month, International Creativity Month, National Hot Tea Month, National Glaucoma Awareness Month
February	AMD Low Vision Awareness Month
May	Older Americans Month, Senior Citizens Month, Senior Health and Fitness Day
September	Adult Day Services Week, Assisted Living Week, Centarians Day, Older Workers Employment Week, Healthy Aging Month, Grandparents Day
November	Family Caregivers Month

WHERE TO BEGIN

When you contact the Area Agency on Aging to find out about the senior population in your area, ask them to give you a list of agencies already serving seniors. Then call, visit or write to tell those agencies you are building a Senior Information Center at your library and would like to include their literature. You are taking a first step in building a relationship by doing something for that agency that will cost the library very little and will benefit your patrons. While you are communicating with them, ask what kind of programming they do, if they have a speaker list, and what topics they cover. Do they recommend books to their clients that would be good additions to the library collection? Do you have meeting rooms they can use for free? Can you put up posters on a community bulletin board or include articles in your library newsletter or on the library Web site to promote their services? Extend the library's free services to an outside agency to show them the value you can offer to a partnership.

Next, contact the local civic organizations that do service projects to help the community. Ask what each group does for the community's senior population. Churches and synagogues, the United Way, the American Red Cross, the Salvation Army, and Scout troops all develop services for seniors. Is there something the library can offer these groups that will make a mutually beneficial partnership? Many local businesses depend on senior customers and may be willing to contribute expertise, resources, gift certificates, and merchandise for senior programs.

Talking to the right person and the same representative of each agency each time you call will help establish open and productive communication. When you have gathered information about the community and know about each organization's expertise, you have already become a valuable knowledgeable resource for the seniors in your library, and you have informed the agencies of your interest in serving the senior population.

Brainstorm with your Senior Advisory Board about program topics that seniors would like that need the expertise of an outside agency. Once you have a list of ideas, go through them with a practical eye to find a doable, unique first program you can offer with a partner you feel very comfortable approaching. Call or visit the potential partner to give an initial presentation of the program idea and to demonstrate how it would be a mutually beneficial partnership. Arrange a meeting time over lunch or coffee at the library to discuss more details. Allow time for the partner to inform his or her agency of the partnership idea.

Once a program idea is agreeable to both partners, list what each partner has to contribute to the program and set a target date for the program and dates for planning meetings. Invite all the persons who will be participating to the planning meetings and ask someone to record minutes so decisions are in writing and everyone understands the plan. Decide who will oversee expenses, publicity, speakers, program space, handouts, refreshments, displays, hostesses, and special equipment. Write a letter of agreement for all partners and be sure to fulfill your part of the partnership to establish trust. When the program is over, remember to say thank you and stay in touch!

PARTNERSHIPS IN ACTION

LIBRARY PARTNERS WITH AARP

Many libraries in the states have offered "55 Alive" refresher driving classes in cooperation with AARP. The instructor talks about changes in vision, hearing, and reaction as they relate to driving, the effects of medications on driving skills, new laws, and tips for hazardous driving conditions. The library provides a meeting area, refreshments and takes registration for the classes. The class runs for two days, four hours each day. Bethel Park Public Library offers the class three times a year. AARP provides the instructor and class materials for a $10.00 fee per student, and couples over fifty-five receive a discount on their car insurance after taking the course. Individuals over fifty-five may also complete the course and receive a discount if they are the sole name on their insurance policy. See www.aarp.org/55alive/about.html for more information about "55 Alive" driving classes and contact your local AARP representative about hosting classes.

Idaho State Library partners with the AARP for "Check Up on Your Prescriptions @ Your Library." The pilot programs were so successful that now more sessions are being hosted throughout Idaho. AARP lined up pharmacists and volunteers to run the program, the library prepared to host the program, and both partners worked on publicity that included fliers, public service announcements, newspaper articles, and radio and cable TV announcements. State legislators were invited to the program. The librarian begins the program with a ten minute review of the medical resources available at the library, the AARP chapter member presents a fifteen minute overview of the pharmaceutical and medical industry, and the pharmacist speaks for fifteen minutes on how to save money on prescriptions. After a short question and answer session, patrons sign up for a one-on-one consultation with the pharmacist. AARP provided lighted pens, pill boxes, printed material, and light refreshments, and the library provided the meeting place and handed out bookmarks. Evaluation forms from the program indicated that almost half of the participants had visited the library for the first time that day! AARP benefited by having a credible host for the program.

LIBRARY PARTNERS WITH HEALTH AND SAFETY PROFESSIONALS

The first wealth is health.

—Ralph Waldo Emerson

A Senior Health Fair at the library might help your community arm seniors with information to help keep them safe and healthy. Fairs take a lot of organization ahead of time, but the participants provide a treasury of information and expertise at one time and in one place, an invaluable convenience for seniors. Invite representatives from health-related businesses and agencies to man tables where seniors can browse, ask questions, and pick up information. Ask the health department and health professionals to provide free blood pressure, diabetes, and glaucoma checks and have safety agencies like the emergency squad and fire department provide information on avoiding and dealing with injuries and accidents. Ask civic organizations to donate items like smoke and carbon monoxide detectors for door prizes.

Long term care is a concern for seniors who may be caring for their own elderly parents or looking for suitable care for themselves should it become necessary. Invite a community outreach nurse to address caregiving and its implications for families with stress management strategies to avoid caregiver burnout. Ask representatives from area nursing homes to discuss expectations, options, possible problems and solutions, and financing and insurance issues.

A series of health programs may suit your library and community. Invite health professionals to speak on topics concerning senior health issues like nutrition, exercise, arthritis, foot care, and stress. Alternative medicine, natural remedies, massage, and aromatherapy are interesting topics as well.

- A physical therapist can bring adaptive equipment for hands-on experience or offer a massage and aromatherapy workshop. Invite participants to bring a massage partner!

- Emergency personnel or the American Red Cross can demonstrate first aid and CPR, giving instruction on how to treat burns, cuts, and choking and how to recognize heart attack symptoms.

- A household safety workshop can help seniors identify and eliminate security and health hazards and give tips for identifying people at the door. Speakers can demonstrate installation and maintenance of smoke and carbon monoxide detectors, give advice on establishing an emergency exit route, provide lessons on self-defense, and guide the audience in adopting attitudes that will minimize risks.

- A mental health counselor can speak on every day stress management and lead the group in exercises with relaxation music.

Richmond Public Library partners with the British Columbia Safety Council to present the "55 Alive" driver training seminars for Canadian seniors, and the Safety Council discounts the fee for the library-hosted classes from $75.00 to $45.00 for the two half day sessions.

The Ohio Senior Health Insurance Information Program (OSHIIP) has been working with Ohio's Public Libraries to educate senior Ohioans about Medicare by distributing over 300 copies of the OSHIIP *Senior Internet Guide,* a publication to help the novice senior surf the Internet for sites about Medicare, along with over 2000 flyers for homebound patrons through library outreach services. OSHIIP also conducts seminars about Medicare and Long Term Insurance at Ohio public libraries.

The Hennepin County Public Library has partnered successfully with several community agencies to produce informative and helpful health programs for seniors. The program "Affordable Prescription Drugs" featured speakers from the Hennepin County Coordinated Home Services and Hennepin County Economic Assistance who explained the drug assistance programs available in the state. For a "Fall Prevention" program, a physical therapist from Intrepid Home Care spoke to participants about risk factors, staying safe and preventing falls.

The library also presented "Options for Seniors," a series of three free programs in celebration of National Senior Citizens Month. For "Long Term Care," a consultant with experience in developing, managing, and evaluating health and human service programs for special needs populations presented information about long term care options. Her work focuses in development and funding of community alternatives for such programs. A social worker from the Minnesota Area Agency on Aging and Senior Linkage Line spoke about affordable and safe housing options in a program titled "Senior Housing Options." "Healthy Eating" was presented by a registered dietician and a chef from the Art Institutes International Minnesota who presented information on how seniors may improve health through better eating habits.

Richmond Public Library partners with Vancouver Coastal Health Authority to present "Living a Healthy Life with Chronic Conditions," a six week health promotion course held for one and a half hours each. The programs are free and limited to card holders, encouraging many people to sign up for library cards.

The Allegheny County Library Association and the Blue Cross partner to sponsor book groups at senior residences. The library association purchases the books and routes them through the local delivery system to the branch library that will deliver the books to the residence. After the discussion is held, the books are routed to another residence or library that will use them for another discussion group.

The Hennepin County Gerontology Alliance sponsored a speaker from the Community Health Department to explain to seniors at several county branches the Five Wishes Program—a living will that allows you to say exactly how you wish to be treated if you become seriously ill. After the program was explained, participants were guided through the steps to fill out the form.

LIBRARY PARTNERS WITH LEGAL AND FINANCIAL PROFESSIONALS

Legal and financial security are important issues for retired and soon-to-be retired patrons. Free programs at the library can inform them of their options and provide them with useful resources. Invite bankers, lawyers, financial advisors, and AARP representatives to give presentations of accurate and current information. Ask the speakers to bring handouts if they have them available, and ask for extras to put in your information center. Allow time for questions and display relevant library materials.

The Tiffin-Seneca Public Library presented "The People's Law School," a series of programs about legal issues featuring visiting judges, attorneys, and the prosecutor discussing topics such as the Court System; Prosecution and Criminal Law; Family Law; Buying, Selling, and Leasing Real Estate; Criminal Defense and the Defendant's Constitutional Rights; Choosing the Proper Business Entity for Your Small Business; and Estate Planning and Probating Decedents' Estates. Other legal issues that could be addressed are elder abuse, health insurance counseling, grandparent rights, protective services, citizenship, and long-term care. Offering the different issues in a series allows seniors to pick and choose the programs they want to attend to get the information they need. The library compiled a bibliography of law-related holdings as a handout.

Help seniors protect themselves from identity theft and con artist scams that target the elderly by presenting programs that help them avoid being victims and tell them what to do if they become victims. Invite speakers from the police department, district attorney's office, Securities Division, Attorney General's office, Federal Trade Commission, or Better Business Bureau. Show the video *Senior Alert* and ask the police department or local law enforcement agency to bring a patrol car, and police dogs to view and talk about neighborhood watches and how the department works.

The trouble with retirement is that you never get a day off.

—Abe Lemons

Pre-Retirement Seminars will empower those seniors approaching retirement. Invite representatives from the Social Security Administration, RSVP and other volunteer groups, Medicare, your community resources, and continuing education organizations to speak and answer questions.

- A representative from the Veteran's Administration can speak to a veteran audience and their families about getting their entitled benefits.
- Present a program focusing on women's retirement issues and government policies.

Seniors have to learn to think of their financial security in a different way after working all their adult lives and receiving regular paychecks. Offer a program that will explain all about nest eggs, including stocks, bonds, annuities, IRAs, mutual funds, and savings accounts. Invite professionals like an AARP representative, a financial advisor, or an investment banker to speak and give advice.

More and more retirees are going back to work, not always out of need, but often to try something new or because they aren't ready to leave the work force. A Senior Job Fair can help these seniors land an interesting second career and a new income. Invite area businesses who hire seniors to set up tables for an open house style program and ask them to bring applications and job descriptions. Gather speakers who can talk about interviewing, resumes, networking and cover letters. Ask representatives from Green Thumb, AARP, EEOC, and the Department of Health and Senior Services to talk and man tables. Have book displays and handouts available and ask area businesses to donate door prizes.

Already a repository for income tax forms, the public libraries can also be a center for seniors to get income tax help from IRS representatives trained to help those over sixty prepare their taxes for free. The library's role is to provide a quiet place to work and to schedule the appointments.

LIBRARY PARTNERS WITH LOCAL AGENCIES

County Extension Services offer several programs that can be presented in cooperation with the library. The Ohio State University Extension Office pairs up seniors and youth for a series of five sessions. The sessions are held once a month and last one and a half to two hours. The first session is an orientation with a discussion for the seniors and an activity booklet for the teens. The second session focuses on nutrition, pairing seniors with teens to make snacks, play bingo, share memories, and talk about how food preparation has changed. Exercise is the topic for the third session, which includes new dance steps, swing dance lessons, low impact aerobics, and a discussion about what it was like going to a dance when you were growing up. Information technology, from radio to the Internet is explored in the fourth session, with discussion about the changes in how news is received. The last session is a field trip to a destination the group chooses together. The pairs can exchange addresses if they would like to continue communicating with each other.

Toronto Public Library partners with the Volunteer Centre of Toronto to host a Senior Volunteer Showcase to connect seniors with community agencies that need volunteers for one time, short term, or long term opportunities. The library and Volunteer Centre partner for another program called the ABCs of Fraud, which teaches seniors to protect themselves against fraud by learning about the latest scams in the community.

Yuma County Library and Meals and Wheels work together for a "Meals on Wheels Library Partnership" to reach new segments of the population. To begin the program, the library sent an introductory letter, an application for homebound service, and a reading interest survey to 180 Meals on Wheels recipients through their volunteers. The homebound patrons are now served reading materials with their Meals on Wheels! The Meals on Wheels volunteers pick up and return materials to the library for the homebound patrons.

Senior Fairs gather many community resources for an afternoon at the library. The Outreach Services Department of Loudon County Public Library participates in an Annual Senior and Caregivers Expo. In a similar event, the Henry County Library invites all groups that work with or provide services to seniors to participate in a four-hour afternoon event. The last fair hosted fifty-two booths and attracted 350 seniors. Participants included six politicians, four financial institutions, three assisted living facilities/nursing homes, twelve other health related businesses, six insurance agencies, twenty government agencies, a law firm with information about Elder Fraud, the Wolfner Library for the Blind and Physically Handicapped, a closet organizing company, the Attorney General's Office's No Call Program, and state agencies. Four of the booths were library related: demonstrations of e-greetings, Internet lessons, fun things to do with grandchildren, and library services for seniors. No political campaign materials were allowed. Goody bags of giveaways donated by the partners were given at the door and attendees could register for door prizes donated by area businesses. The Friends of the Library hosted a lemonade stand with cookies. An information station displayed literature from businesses unable to attend.

The Toledo-Lucas Public Library partners with several community agencies like Toledo Legal Aid, the American Red Cross, and the Social Security Administration to present a community-wide forum for grandparents. The program presents needed information, resources, and community connections for grandparents.

LIBRARY PARTNERS WITH LOCAL BUSINESSES

North Canton Public Library partnered with local businesses to bring in Peter Alsop, a nationally known children's singer-songwriter, to give concerts for the community.

The St. Louis County Library partnered with a local sponsor to create a "Senior Reading Club." The goal was to encourage reading among the outreach patrons and to provide a way for seniors to carry their reading material. Canvas tote bags were purchased by the library and a sponsor for all the participants who read twenty books for the program. Six hundred ninety-one seniors accomplished the goal.

The Gates Public Library and Rochester Free-net teamed up to sponsor the Senior S.I.G. (Special Interest Group), a group that meets for two hours each month to discuss and practice Internet skills. Senior Clubs sponsored by the Town of Gates Recreation Department also receive instruction on a computer set aside for their own use.

LIBRARY PARTNERS WITH BOOK DISCUSSION GROUPS

Independent book discussion groups find the library a logical place to meet. Toronto Public Library hosts a Feminist Book Discussion Group for the North York Chapter of the Older Women's Network that meets one Sunday each month to share views and ideas about selected books on feminist issues for older women.

The Seniors' Literary Circle invites a librarian from Richmond Public Library to talk about fiction, writing, and library services and collections. The group produces a collection of poetry and short fiction called *Perceptions,* which the library catalogues and adds to the collection.

LIBRARY PARTNERS WITH COUNTY FAIRS

Tiffin-Seneca Public Library participates each July in "Seniors Day at the Seneca County Fair," a full day of activities planned just for seniors. Your library can conduct a card campaign, distribute giveaways, recruit volunteers, and have door prize drawings at the county fair!

LIBRARY PARTNERS WITH CHARITY

The library is perceived to be a neutral meeting place for all people, and therefore is an excellent forum for services for the public. For example, Loudonville Public Library houses the Golden Center, administered by the Catholic Charities and dedicated to the senior patrons, which provides programs, hot lunches, and computers set aside for the seniors.

PARTNER BANKS

All of the partnerships in this chapter were formed with the common goal of benefiting the senior audience. Listed below are some of the many organizations that focus on services for seniors or have developed programs for seniors. Find out which of these agencies are your neighbors and potential partners:

- AAA: The mission of the Area Agency on Aging is to provide services which make it possible for older individuals to remain in their own homes, preserving their independence and dignity. www.n4a.org.

- AARP: American Association of Retired Persons is a nonprofit, nonpartisan membership organization for people fifty and over. www.aarp.org.

- NARFE: The National Association of Retired Federal Employees is dedicated to protecting the earned retirement benefits of federal employees, retirees and their survivors. www.narfe.org.

- RSVP: Retired and Senior Volunteer Program provides older Americans the opportunity to apply their life experience to meeting community needs. www.seniorcorps.org/joining/rsvp.

- SPRY: Setting Priorities for Retirement Years Foundation. http://spry.org.

- Gray Panthers: Gray Panthers sponsors consciousness raising and educational programs. www.gray-panthers.org.

- Elderhostel: Elderhostel is a not-for-profit organization dedicated to providing extraordinary learning adventures for people fifty-five and over. www.elderhostel.org.

- Community senior centers

- Council of senior citizens

- Senior community service employment programs

- Foster grandparent programs

- Adult day care centers

- Nursing homes

- Lifecare communities

- Local colleges

- Alumni groups

- Service organizations

- Senior residences

- Senior nutrition sites
- Churches and synagogues
- Community centers
- Social service agencies

RESOURCES

FOR OVERVIEW:

1. Abrams, Anne. 2002. "Partnership with AARP Was Our State Library's Prescription for Success." *MLS* 16, Nos. 6 & 7. (September/October): 1–3.

2. Institute of Museum and Library Services (IMLS). www.imls.gov/about/index.htm.

3. Missouri State Library. *Serving Seniors: A Resource Manual for Missouri Libraries.* www.sos.state.mo.us/library/development/services /seniors/manual/default.asp.

FOR HEALTH AND SAFETY PROGRAMS:

1. Davis, Ruth. 1999. *The Nursing Home Handbook: A Guide to Living Well.* Holbrook, MA: Adams Media.

2. Harteau, Janee, and Holly Keegal. 1999. *A Senior's Guide to Personal Safety.* Minneapolis: Fairview Press.

3. Shelton, Phyllis R. 1998. *Long Term Care Planning Guide: The Consumer Resource for Long-Term Care Financing.* Nashville: Shelton Marketing Services.

4. "AARP." www.aarp.org.

5. "National Association of Area Agency on Aging." www.n4a.org.

6. Ohio Senior Health Insurance Information Program (OSHIIP). www.ohioinsurance.gov.

7. *Crime: Senior Alert.* 1989. 2nd ed. Gordon-Kerckhoff Productions. AIMS Media. Videocassette.

FOR LEGAL AND FINANCIAL SECURITY PROGRAMS:

1. Harkness, Helen. 1999. *Don't Stop the Career Clock.* Palo Alto, CA: Davies-Black.

2. VGM Career Horizons, eds. 2000. *Resumes for Mid-Career Job*

Changes, 2nd ed. Lincolnwood, Ill.: VGM Career Horizons.

    3. AARP. "Money and Work." www.aarp.org/indexes/money.html.

    4. Experience Works: Senior Workforce Solutions. www.experi enceworks.org/index.html.

    5. Federal Trade Commission Home Page. www.ftc.gov.

    6. Federal Trade Commision. "ID Theft." www.consumer.gov/ idtheft.

    7. Quackwatch. www.quackwatch.com.

FOR PARTNER BANKS:

    1. Missouri State Library. "Agencies Providing Services on Aging." *Serving Seniors: A Resource Manual for Missouri Libraries.* www.sos.mo.gov/library/development/services/seniors/manual/default .asp.

    2. American Library Association. "Guidelines for Services to Older Adults." www.ala.org/Content/NavigationMenu/Our_ Association/Offices/Literacy_and_Outreach_Services/Outreach _Resources/elderly.pdf.

6 MIX SENIORS WITH TEENS AND CHILDREN

It's one of nature's ways that we often feel closer to distant generations than to the generation immediately preceding us.

—Igor Stravinsky

OVERVIEW

Bring generations together to strengthen the community at the library with intergenerational programs. America has become highly segregated by age; children, adults, and older adults are all separated into age-specific institutions, from preschools to nursing homes, resulting in stereotypes, misunderstandings, and tension between the generations. Families are often far apart from each other, too, and many children do not benefit from frequent interaction with their grandparents. The library is the perfect meeting place for people of all ages, and an intergenerational program is the perfect setting to bring different generations together for a meaningful and enriching exchange. All generations have something valuable to share with another; young people become more comfortable with and understanding of the changes that come with aging, and seniors enjoy sharing what they know and providing needed unconditional acceptance and companionship for children and teens.

Intergenerational programs also build working relationships between library departments and spread library programming dollars farther by distributing the task of providing the program among more staff members, encouraging more brainstorming creativity, and sharing the preparation workload. Invite a representative from each of the generations you want to participate in the program to a planning meeting where they can give feedback on your ideas and provide suggestions.

Libraries of all sizes create their own successful intergenerational programs, sometimes with very limited funds. Several intergenerational programs utilizing the BiFolkal Kits, which you may already have available to you, are described at the ALA Web site (see resources). These programs are an opportunity for the elders to share their memories with younger participants and can be presented at the library or a senior facility. BiFolkal also offers videos and program guides for establishing an intergenerational visiting program. The Coshocton Public Library has had success with its Grand Time @ the Library and Grandparents Day programs.

Seniors and young people mix well and tend to have a good time with the programs described in this chapter. Try one of the programs to celebrate National Intergenerational Week in May. From hosting a reception to starting a Veteran's History Project, there is something for libraries of all sizes and all budgets.

SENIORS WITH CHILDREN

RECEPTION FOR NATIONAL LIBRARY WEEK

What better way to celebrate National Library Week than by honoring your youngest and oldest library patrons with a reception! Ask family members to invite other members of family and friends to the celebration, present a book as a gift to the two honored guests, and serve cake and punch for everyone. The local newspaper can take pictures and interview both patrons (maybe the mother of the youngest!), providing a wonderful photo opportunity and a human interest story illustrating how the public library enriches all stages of life.

COMBINED STORY TIMES

Bring the very young and the elderly together for story times. Invite children from an on-site day care or the preschool story group to come to a nursing home for an occasional combined program or story time. Let the children sit on the floor in front of the seated residents so they can interact. The picture books in the booklists in Appendix E will appeal to all ages. The outreach coordinator and the children's department can work together to tell stories, lead songs and finger plays, and create an easy craft. Lead the children in singing a song they know for the residents. The residents will enjoy the energy and the smiles of the young children, whom they may not get an opportunity to see very often. Older children can help pass around handouts, bookmarks, and crafts.

BOOK BUDDIES PROGRAMS

Book Buddies is a program that can combine any two generations for a story sharing time. Seniors can be matched with children for a one-on-one story time at the library. The focus is enjoying books and reading and is not intended to be a tutoring program. Recruit senior volunteers to train for the program before asking parents to register their children, and ask seniors when they are available so you can match a senior with a child. Book Buddies programs can be ongoing programs if enough volunteers are available, but a shorter-term Book Buddy program—a summer program, for example—can be concluded with a recognition party. The age range of participating children can be limited if there are many more children than volunteers. For the children's safety, make ID badges for the library grandparent volunteers and keep the reading site in a public area in view of the on duty staff.

A model for an ongoing program can be found at the Los Angeles Public Library, where "Grandparents and Books" has been a successful after school and summer reading program for over ten years. An online training manual describing the basic program and ideas for enhancement with extra supplies and services is available in pdf format for library grandparents who want to read to young children at www.lapl.org/admin/gab.html. Volunteers fill out applications and attend training sessions to learn how to choose books, interact with children, and schedule reading times. Training session outlines, application forms, instructions for telling flannel board stories, and other tips for storytelling are included in the online manual.

Match children aged six and up with seniors in a mystery series program. The senior volunteers read two "Encyclopedia Brown" books at each session and the children are invited to solve the mystery before the solution is read at the end of the story.

New readers benefit from a Book Buddy program held over the summer months. Match up first and second graders with seniors and promote the program through the schools in the spring. The children and volunteers can read to each other for one hour a week. Provide incentive sheets and stickers for the senior to award the child when reading assignments are completed. Ask the Friends of the Library to provide gift certificates to a local book store for the children and seniors who complete the program.

Train seniors to do story times at child care centers using theme kits from the children's department that make building a story time a simple task. Picture books, songs on audiotapes, flannel board stories, realia objects, poems, and finger plays about one theme are collected in a container for checkout. Give the storytellers some easy tips for doing a good story time: be familiar with the materials, sit or stand a little higher than the children, read loudly enough and slowly, and show the children the pictures as you read.

GRANDPARENTS DAY CELEBRATIONS

Grandparents Day, celebrated on the first Sunday after Labor Day in September, is a perfect occasion for a first intergenerational program. Marian McQuade, a housewife in Fayette County, West Virginia, originated this holiday to persuade grandchildren to tap the wisdom and heritage their grandparents could provide. She began a campaign in 1973

Figure 6-1 Photos, books and props that fit the Grandparent's Day program theme make an eye-catching display.

to set aside a day for grandparents and in 1978, President Jimmy Carter proclaimed National Grandparents Day a yearly holiday.

The library can provide Grandparents Day programs that are opportunities for grandparents to spend quality time with their grandchildren. The children's department and the outreach/senior adult department can work together to make these events possible. Many libraries take advantage of the generous yearly $300.00 Grandparents Day Grant that is awarded by Wal-Mart to a nonprofit organization in the community for the benefit of senior adults. For more information about this grant, click on "what we fund" at www.walmartfoundation.org. Call a local Wal-Mart store to ask for information and an application by the end of July each year. The Friends of the Library are also a great source for funding Grandparents Day programs and can volunteer to help at the program. Also, call your state library and ask what funds are available for intergenerational programs.

Publicize a Grandparents Day program with flyers at the main circulation desk and in the children's room in the library, articles in the library newsletter and the local newspaper, and public service announcements at the radio station. An announcement in church and synagogue bulletins and posters at senior centers, Laundromats, and groceries will reach many more seniors. Pictures of staff members when they were young with their grandparents, pictures of those who attended previous programs, and items and books that fit the theme can be put in a display case to publicize this event.

Here are some tips to help you plan a successful Grandparents Day program:

- Start planning early with the children's department staff. Choose a theme for the program; select books, activities, and decorations for the room; and discuss budget allowance, favors for the attendees, time and length of the program, and the refreshments. Decide what each department will do.

- Use leftover summer reading prizes as favors for the children.

- Set the date and time of the program and begin publicity.

- Require registration and decide if the attendance will need to be limited. Include this information in the publicity. Registration will help with the final plans for food and craft supplies/favors and for making place cards so families can sit together.

- Play music as guests arrive and sign up for door prizes.
- Take pictures! It is nice to have one other staff member who will be responsible for taking candid pictures to use in a scrapbook and as publicity for future events and projects. Provide photo release forms at the program.
- Take turns reading the books and poems. The change keeps the children's attention and they can also participate in the story by joining in choruses.
- Send thank you notes to anyone who provided funds, food, or other materials for the programs.

Figure 6-2 Remember to give your audience model release forms so you can use the photos for publicizing upcoming programs and services at the library.

The Library
Model's Release Form

I hereby grant to the Library and anyone authorized by the organization the right to copyright, reproduce, publish, and otherwise use my photograph and my name in any and all media, for purposes of advertising and promoting libraries and literacy.

Print Name /Age _____

Signature _____

Address _____

Phone Number _____

Date _____

Witness (Parent or guardian if under 18) _____

ADOPT A GRAND!

Present a program for seniors and children that don't have grandparents nearby; invite nursing home residents to the library and children from the local community. Make several kinds of buttons for the guests, two of each kind. One of the pair is for a senior, the other for a child. As the guests arrive, give them all a button. The persons wearing matching buttons find each other and are adopted grands for the program! Several stories and activities work well for this program:

- Make introductions and provide a brief history of Grandparents Day.
- Acknowledge businesses who donated to the program.
- Play "Warm Up" from *Preschool Favorites* by Georgiana Stewart.
- Read *It's Not My Turn to Look for Grandma!* by April Halprin Wayland.
- Play a memory game. A tray of twenty items is passed around for a few minutes to study. Paper and pencils are distributed and the tray is covered. The teams try to remember and write down what was on the tray.
- Play "Bendable Stretchable" from *Preschool Favorites*.
- Play "Finger Poppin" from *Preschool Favorites*.
- Read *The Very Noisy Night* by Diana Hendry.
- Read *Grandpa's Song* by Tony Johnston.
- Sing "Best Song in the World" from *Grandpa's Song*.
- Serve cracked cake from *Grandpa's Song*.

TREAT YOUR GRANDPARENTS LIKE ROYALTY

Children can treat their own grandparents like royalty by inviting them to a program at the library. There are several stories and activities that fit a royal theme:

- Make introductions and provide a brief history of Grandparents Day.
- Acknowledge businesses who donated to the program.
- Read *The King, the Mice and the Cheese* by Nancy Gurney
- Read *If I Were Queen of the World* by Fred Hiatte.
- Play "The King Commands" game (Simon Says).
- Make a crown craft.

- Make a cheese and crackers snack.
- Create a family coat of arms.

GRANDPARENTS DAY AT THE LIBRARY

Allow about one hour for this program. Place pots of mums in the center of each table for door prizes and put napkins, plates, and cups for each guest on each side of the flowers. Include materials to make the activity booklets at each grandchild's place setting: markers, crayons, pencils, the five pages described below, and ribbon for tying the booklet together. Place an acrylic frame with a printed verse at each grandparent's setting. Here are some stories and activities for this program:

- Make introductions and provide a brief history of Grandparents Day.
- Acknowledge businesses who donated to the program.
- Read the poem "What Is a Grandma?" by Barbara Cage http://home.earthlink.net/~ncoleman1/poems.html.
- Read *Grandmother's Chair* by Ann Herbert Scott.
- Read *What, Cried Granny! an Almost Bedtime Story* by Kate Lum.
- Complete the activity booklet described below.
- Serve doughnut holes, pumpkin cookies, cider, and pretzels.
- Award door prizes.

The Activity Booklet

You can create this activity booklet from the www.grandparchild-day.com Web site quickly on a word processor or desktop publishing program. Make a copy of each page for each grand couple and punch holes along one edge for a ribbon tie.

- The cover: Print "Grandparents Day" and the date of the program. To decorate the cover, the child traces the grandparent's hand, then the grandchild and grandparent can trace the child's hand inside the grandparent's outline, "hand in hand." Crayons or markers are used to make the handprints.

- Page 2: Print "Memories," and list questions for the child to ask their grandparent, leaving spaces to write the answers. Samples of the questions to use are: When and where were you born? What were your favorite games and activities when you were a child? What was your favorite book when you were a child? Did you have a pet?
- Page 3: Print "My Family Tree," and a family tree outline for the grandparent to help the child fill in and learn about their family.
- Page 4: Print "My Grandparent and Me" and leave space for the child to draw a picture.
- Page 5: Print "Created with love by…," and leave space for the grandparent and child to fill in their names.
- Assemble the pages in order and tie with a ribbon.

Framed Verses Keepsake

Make a keepsake for the grandparents. Purchase small acrylic picture frames and use a publisher program to add a pretty border or clip art to a verse such as "Grandchildren have a special way of bringing joy to every day."

GRANDPARENTS AND GRANDCHILDREN ARE SOUPER!

When grandparents register for this program, give each of them a form to submit a favorite recipe and set a deadline to allow time to assemble the recipes into a booklet entitled "Grand Recipes for Our Grandchildren." Make copies as keepsake favors for each guest.

Allow one hour for this program. Place potted mums in the center of each table for door prizes and place a can of soup ingredients at each place setting. Place peanut butter and jelly sandwiches and cheese and crackers in baskets at each table with bowls, spoons, and napkins. There are several stories and activities appropriate for this program:

- Make introductions and a provide short history of Grandparents Day.
- Acknowledge businesses who donated to the program.
- Read *Grandpa's Soup* by Eiko Kadono and provide a soup making activity.

- Read *Stone Soup: An Old Tale* by Marcia Brown.
- Read *The Gingerbread Man* by Eric A. Kimmel and provide a cookie decorating activity.
- Award door prizes and distribute recipe booklets.

Grandpa's Soup takes place in Grandpa's kitchen, where he is trying to prepare the same soup his wife used to make. Each day he makes a new batch of soup, remembering a few more of the ingredients and every day someone shows up at his door and helps him eat the soup. The book includes a recipe for Grandpa's Soup, which you can make before the program. A second empty pot can be placed on a cart and wheeled down the center of the room as *Grandpa's Soup* is read. The children add each ingredient to the soup pot to act out the story. After the story, serve the prepared soup and read *Stone Soup: An Old Tale*.

Read *The Gingerbread Man* after the soup supper and ask everyone to join in the chorus. Pass out gingerbread boy cutout cookies with a small tube of frosting and a tiny box of raisins for the children to decorate for dessert.

GRANDPARENTS AND GRANDCHILDREN ARE WINNERS

In this program, grandparents share some of the games they played when they were young with their grandchildren while enjoying some old fashioned refreshments. Borrow a variety of classic children's games: Dominoes, Pick Up Sticks, Parcheesi, Tic Tac Toe, Checkers, Old Maid, Go Fish, Crazy Eights, Candyland, and Chutes and Ladders. Staff members involved in the program may join in the games, encourage the players, and refill refreshments. There are several stories and activities for this program:

- Make introductions and provide a short history of Grandparents Day.
- Acknowledge businesses who donated to the program.
- Read *The Relatives Came* by Cynthia Rylant.
- Read *The Berenstain Bears and the Week at Grandma's* by Stan and Jan Berenstain.
- Play old fashioned games.
- Hold a photo session.
- Serve pretzels, popcorn, sugar wafer cookies, and root beer floats.

During the games, each family is invited by the photographer to go to the children's room for a digital photo posed with the child's favorite book. When all the photos are taken, print two iron-on transfers of each photo with the caption "Reading is Grand" under the picture. Give book bags to the children and aprons to the grandparents with the iron-ons and a copy of the ironing directions. The Dharma Trading Company catalog (www.dharmatrading.com) was an inexpensive and reliable source for the canvas book bags and aprons our library distributed. The cost of the book bags is $1.69 each for one to one hundred and the aprons are $3.95 each for thirty-six or more. Iron-on transfer paper can be purchased at Wal-Mart or an office supply store.

Figure 6-3 Photographs help preserve memories and when used as an iron-on, makes an apron, t-shirt, or book bag a special keepsake.

RED, WHITE, AND BLUE AND YOU!

Red, White, Blue and You! celebrates America with red, white, and blue decorations, patriotic stories, hot dogs, and apple pie. Ask a local business to donate small flags to give to all the participants, ask McDonalds to donate apple pies, and ask another fast food restaurant to donate condiments. Order the following items from the Oriental Trading Company (www.orientaltrading.com): patriotic teddy bears, candy wrapped in patriotic wrappers, patriotic pencils, Uncle Sam note pads, and red and white checked tablecloths. Here are the story and activity ideas for this program:

- Make introductions and provide a short history of Grandparents Day.
- Acknowledge businesses who donated to the program.
- Serve hot dogs, buns, potato chips, carrots and dip.
- Read *God Bless America/Irving Berlin* illustrated by Lynn Munsinger.
- Read *America Is...* by Louise Borden.
- Read *The Flag We Love* by Pam Munoz Ryan.
- Sing *This Land Is Your Land* by Woodie Guthrie.
- Distribute newspapers to make newspaper hats.
- Distribute small flags.
- Lead a march through the library, wearing hats, waving flags, and playing a march on a portable cassette player.
- Distribute favors.

GRANDPARENTS RAISING GRANDCHILDREN

According to the 2000 US Census, 2,350,477 grandparents are responsible for raising one or more of their grandchildren, and the numbers of children in grandparent-headed households have increased 30 percent since 1990. These families face special challenges involving legal, financial, child care, medical care, emotional, and educational decisions. The statistics for your own state and fact sheets with state-specific services available to custodial grandparents can be found at www.childrensdefense.org. Many more grandparents baby-sit their grandchildren while parents are working.

Libraries can be information centers for these caregivers, offering publications and programs where they can connect with others and find support. A free subscription to *Parenting Grandchildren: A Voice for Grandparents,* a quarterly newsletter published by AARP's Grandparent Information Center, is available at www.aarp.org/grandparents or by calling (800) 424–3410. The Web sites listed in the resources are helpful to share with custodial grandparents and are a valuable resource for program planners. A flyer or bookmark with the addresses for these sites can be distributed at grandparent programs, made available in the library's Senior Information Center, and given to senior centers.

Supportive programs like "Grand Time @ the Library" help these grandparents connect with each other as well as provide an environment for quality relaxed time with their grandchildren. Agencies that may collaborate with libraries for this type of programming include the local Council on Aging, AARP, and Volunteers of America.

GRAND TIME @ THE LIBRARY

Figure 6-4 Grand Time @ the Library Poster

Figure 6-5 The Red Round House story

The Red Round House
(Adapted)

Once there was a little boy who went to visit his grandma. He was getting restless, so Grandma told him to go out on her farm and find a red round house with no doors and no windows and a star inside.

He first met his cousin.

"Do you know where I can find a red round house with no doors, no windows, and a star inside?"

"No," said his cousin, "I've never heard of that kind of house. Why don't you ask Farmer Jones?"

So the little boy looked for Farmer Jones.

"Farmer Jones," said the little boy, "have you ever seen a red round house with no doors and no windows and a star inside?"

"No," said Farmer Jones, "I've never heard of that kind of house. Why don't you ask my wife in the orchard over there?"

So the little boy skipped over to the orchard to look for Farmer Jones' wife. He didn't see Farmer Jones' wife, but just then the wind blew an apple out of a tree and it fell at his feet. Out of the apple crawled a tiny little worm!

"Hmmm…" thought the boy. "This apple is the little worm's house. It is red and round and has no doors or windows, but I don't see any star!"

He took the apple home to his Grandma and asked, "Could this be the red round house with no doors and no windows?"

"Yes, it is!" said his Grandma. "Good job!"

"But Grandma, where is the star?" asked the little boy.

And Grandma cut the apple in half to show him the star inside.

(Cut an apple in half crosswise so that the children can see the star)

"Grand Time @ the Library" is an opportunity for children grades K-6 and their grandparents to meet once a month for an hour of stories, interactive projects, and snacks. It allows grandparents and their grand-children to work and play together, share hobbies, and make crafts in a relaxed atmosphere. Hand out a laminated bookmark with the dates for all the Grand Time Programs for the year to the children and the seniors and send a reminder post card each month to the participants. Choose a different theme for each program and display books relating to the theme for browsing and checkout. The program themes with materials and activities listed below will inspire more ideas.

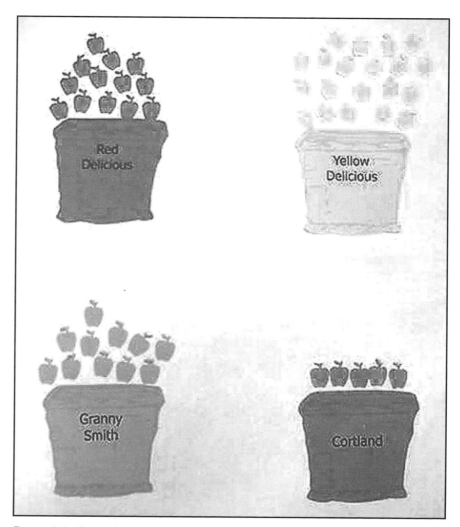

Figure 6-6 Grandchildren vote for their favorite apples by filling the basket they choose.

Figure 6-7 Grandparents and grandchildren enjoy making apple smiles....and eating them!

APPLES

- Provide introductions.
- Read *Johnny Appleseed* by Reeve Lindbergh.
- Read *Red Round House* (see figure 6-5).
- Taste and compare four different kinds of apples.
- Vote for favorite apples (see figure 6-6).
- Make apple smiley faces with apple slices, peanut butter, and miniature marshmallows.
- Use the activity sheets available at www.bestapples.com/kids.

NATIONAL CHILDREN'S BOOK WEEK

- Make introductions.
- Provide a brief history of National Children's Book Week.
- Read *Beverly Billingsly Borrows a Book* by Alexander Stadler.
- Play *What Animal Is In...?* (www.cbcbooks.org/html/book_week_activities.html), a crossword puzzle with book titles for clues. Display the books for solving the puzzle.

- Read *The Library* by Sarah Stewart.
- Make wallpaper journals. Use wallpaper for the cover and plain paper for the pages. Tell the children they can write a book of their own and offer suggestions: things they are thankful for, their own poetry, a story of their own, a picture book with their drawings, a biography, or a journal of pasted pictures from a magazine.
- Read *Twas the Night Before Thanksgiving* by Dav Pilkey.
- Serve doughnuts, pretzels, coffee, and milk.
- Color the sheet from www.cbcbooks.org/mousecolorin.jpg.
- Distribute National Children's Book Week bookmarks and pencils, Thanksgiving stickers, and another crossword puzzle based on authors of books.
- Display books on writing journals and becoming an author for browsing and checkout.

Figure 6-8 Send reminder post cards to the grandparents and grandchildren so they don't miss a Grand Time @ the Library!

You are invited to join
A Grand Time @ the Library
October 21, 2002—6:30-7:30 pm
For children grades K-6 grades and their grandparents
Stories, activities, and snacks to please
the young and young at heart!
We will meet in the large meeting room
the third Monday of each month

Hope to see you there!
The topic for this month is
Apples

THE GIVING TREE

- If there is a Christmas tree in the program room, on the invitation ask the children to bring a pair of mittens to hang on the tree to be given to the Salvation Army or another charity.
- Make introductions.
- Ask the children to tell about their Christmas trees. Ask them if they know what is unique about Christmas trees: they stay green all year.
- Have each person draw a Christmas tree on top of his or her own head on paper with a marker. Show the trees.
- Make green and red paper chains using glue sticks and send home more paper strips to add to the chains.
- Read *The Mitten Tree* by Candace Christiansen
- Have the children hang their mittens on the Christmas tree.
- Read *The Night Tree* by Eve Bunting
- Read *Twas the Night Before Christmas* by Clement Moore with illustrations by Grandma Moses.
- Serve hot chocolate, popcorn, and cookies.
- Sing carols.
- Give handouts: a Christmas tree word search puzzle, bookmarks, and rubber ink stamps in the shape of mittens.

OUR ANIMAL FRIENDS IN WINTER

- Make introductions.
- Read *Stranger in the Woods* by Carl R. Sams II and Jean Stoick, a delightful photographic book about animals that detect a stranger, gather to investigate, and discover the stranger is a snowman built by two children to feed the animals.
- Play the elimination game *Who's the Stranger?* Silently select one of the children to be the stranger and ask everyone to stand. Give descriptive clues about the stranger one at a time, each clue becoming

more specific (the stranger is a boy, the stranger has brown hair, the stranger is wearing blue, etc.). Anyone not matching the clue sits down. Continue until the one child who is the stranger is left standing.

- Make a Symbolic Snowman. Give each person a white sheet of paper and markers and ask them to draw a snowman that tells something about them by following certain steps. For example, boys draw three snowballs for their snowmen and girls draw two. Each person draws the snowman's eyes the same color as their own. If they have ever built a snowman, they draw a dotted mouth. If not, they draw a solid mouth. If the person likes cold weather, they draw a carrot nose. If they like warm weather, a button nose. If they like to play in the snow, they give their snowman a square hat. If not, their snowman gets a stocking hat. They add one button on the snowman's belly for each person in their family.

- Read *The Mitten* by Jan Brett.

- Serve hot chocolate and powdered sugar doughnut holes or snowman shaped cookies

- Make bird feeders. The day before the program, cut bread slices with a snowman cookie cutter, use a straw to make a hole at the top for a yarn hanger, and let it dry. The grandchildren and grandparents add a yarn tie, spread them with peanut butter, and then sprinkle them with bird seed. Provide plastic sandwich bags to carry the snowmen home.

- Read *Bear Snores On* by Karma Wilson and Jane Chapman and let the children join in the chorus.

GRAND TIME FEEDBACK FROM THE GRANDS

- "It's a joy to bring grandchildren David and Anna to the library and share in the various activities with them. Also enjoy the delightful stories that are read from the colorful books." —Lavonne P. (grandparent)

- "I like going to "A Grand Time @ the Library" because of the fun activities, neat books, and wonderful crafts." —Lasha P. (grandchild)

- "I enjoy my time with my granddaughter and listening to the stories with the library people and they also have neat crafts and things to do. We look forward to this time every month. Thank you." —Judy P. (grandparent)

- "We have lots of fun! Great one-on-one time! We make an evening when Grand Time arrives. We go out to dinner before we come to the library. We really enjoy our time together. Coming to Grand Time was Kyle's idea. I'm so glad he chose to share this time with me." —Ann B. (grandparent)

- "I love to spend time with my grandma! We have tons of fun! We always go out to dinner before we come. We have lots of fun." —Kyle T. (grandchild)

- "It gives us an opportunity to interact with each other doing things that are fun that we would not usually do together." —Terry L. L. (grandparent)

- "I like to spend time with my great-granddaughter." —Ivy C. (grandparent)

- "We enjoy time at the library because we share time and books with each other. Introducing the children to books opens so many doors for them. We are also making memories that will last forever." —Wanda U. (grandparent)

- "I like to read books and visit with the librarians." —Chelsey U. (granddaughter)

SENIORS AND TEENS

Is there a school close to the library so a class could come to the library for lunch? Do you have a group of seniors that would enjoy talking to young people and sharing their knowledge and memories? Bring them together to reach across the generations over a lunch discussion once a month. A potluck lunch and a different topic each month and will inspire a lively exchange. Books, family, community, generations, and news events are some of the topics both ages will have in common.

Invite a high school basketball team to visit nursing homes with you and demonstrate ball handling skills, discuss the team's progress during the season, and read short stories. The activities director can lead everyone in exercises so the residents can work out with the team.

Invite teens and seniors to discuss historical topics together several times a year. This informal conversation can cover events the elders have experienced and the teens are studying in school such as D-Day, the Negro Baseball League, and the Holocaust.

Match teen tutors with senior computer students one or two hours a week for fun or to fulfill community service requirements. The teams may decide to continue working together on a regular basis or occasionally when the senior needs assistance. Teach the teens how to work with seniors, how older people learn best, and how to use the library's online resources. Working one-on-one makes scheduling time easier.

Here are more ideas for mixing seniors and teens:

- Host a Poetry Writing Workshop once a month for all ages, children to seniors, so they can mix together and share their common love of poetry.

- Ask teen volunteers to take books to senior care facilities, visit with the residents, read to individual residents, and suggest books.

- Host a hobby workshop that appeals to all ages and ask the seniors to share their expertise with the young hobbyists. Building model trains or collecting stamps are two possibilities.

- Ask Teen Advisory Boards to help with programs at nursing homes and serve refreshments at senior programs.

- Teens can perform Reader's Theatre plays for a senior audience. Each teen reads the lines for a different character and simple props can be used. Audiences can be prompted to add sound effects to the story.

- Organize a "Senior" Prom at a senior center. Invite seniors and high school teens to dress up for a dance and ask seniors to teach the teens swing dance steps and the teens to teach the seniors a modern dance. Provide decorations, music, and refreshments that suit your budget.

- Coordinate a scout troop to videotape interviews with long time community residents for local history stories that can be shown to the public.

- Connect children and Books-By-Mail patrons or teens and nursing home residents as pen pals.

- Coordinate a quilt project with seniors and teens. The seniors pass along a traditional art and the finished project can decorate a wall in the library.

TEEN/SENIOR WEB CONNECTION

SENIORS—
learn how to use the Internet.

TEENS—
we need you to tutor seniors.

www.aclibrary.org

Alameda County LIBRARY
...Infinite possibilities

Figure 6-9 Teen/Senior Web Connection Flyer

VETERAN'S HISTORY PROJECT

The Library of Congress has created a wonderful opportunity to inspire younger generations to capture the memories of the oldest generation. The Veteran's History Project, part of the American Folklife Center, will honor all veterans of World War I, World War II, and the Korean, Vietnam, and Persian Gulf wars and preserve their memories by collecting and preserving audio and video oral histories and documentary materials such as letters, diaries, maps, photographs, and home movies. Contributions of civilian volunteers, support staff, war industry workers, and military personnel from the Air Force, Army, Marine Corps, and Navy, U.S. Coast Guard, and Merchant Marine are documented. The Library of Congress will create a catalog of all the materials collected from the Veteran's History Project and display all the names of the contributing veterans on the American Memory Web site with online presentations of some of the material.

Official Partner organizations are eligible for free training workshops on conducting oral history interviews and documenting with audio and video recordings. Teens can be trained and matched up with veterans to interview or be encouraged to interview a veteran from their own families. A project kit is available at the Web site.

RESOURCES

FOR OVERVIEW

1. American Library Association. "Services to the Elderly, List of Intergenerational Programs." www.ala.org/Content/NavigationMenu/Our_Association/Offices/Literacy_and_Outreach_Services/Outreach_Resources/List_of_Intergenerational_Programs.htm.

FOR SENIORS WITH CHILDREN

1. Los Angeles Public Library. "Grandparents and Books." www.lapl.org/admin/gab.html.

FOR GRANDPARENTS DAY PROGRAMS:

1. The Dharma Trading Company. www.dharmatrading.com.
2. National Grandparents Council. "National Grandparents Day." www.grandparents-day.com.

3. Oriental Trading Company. www.orientaltrading.com.
4. Wal-Mart Good Works. www.walmartfoundation.org.

FOR GRANDPARENTS RAISING GRANDCHILDREN:

1. Grands Place. "For Grandparents and Special Others Raising Grandchildren." www.grandsplace.com.
2. The Grandparent Foundation. "Foundation on Grandparenting." www.grandparenting.org.
3. Grand Parent Again. www.grandparentagain.com.
4. CyberGran. "Grandparent's Web." www.cyberparent.com/gran.
5. AARP Grandparent Information Center. "Parenting Grandchildren: a Voice for Grandparents." www.aarp.org/grandparents.
6. *Surrounded with Love: Grandparents Raising Grandchildren.* 1999. Terra Nova Films, Inc. Videocassette.

FOR NATIONAL CHILDREN'S BOOK WEEK

1. Children's Book Council. "Book Week Activities." www.cbc books.org/html/book_week_activities.html.
2. Children's Book Council. "A History of Children's Book Week." www.cbcbooks.org/html/history.html.
3. Family Crafts. "Wallpaper Books." http://familycrafts.about.com/ cs/homemadebooks/index_2.htm.

FOR OUR ANIMAL FRIENDS IN WINTER

1. Van Beveren, Angela. 2002. "Stranger in the Woods, Written and photo-illustrated by Carl R. Sams II and Jean Stoick." *The Mailbox: The Idea Magazine for Teachers,*. December/January: 30–31.

FOR SENIORS AND TEENS

1. Abramson, Marla. 2002. "Lunch Special." *BOOK,* September/October.
2. The Library of Congress. "American Memory: Historical Collections for the National Digital Library." http://memory.loc.gov.
3. The Library of Congress American Folklife Center. "Veterans History Project: Partners." www.loc.gov/folklife/vets/workshop info.html.
4. The Library of Congress American Folklife Center. "Veteran's History Project: Participate in the Project." www.loc.gov/folklife/vets/ kit.html.

FOR MORE INTERGENERATIONAL PROGRAM IDEAS:

1. Keeshan, Bob. 1994. *Family Fun Activity Book: Playtime and Activities to Bring Children and Grownups Together.* Minneapolis: Deaconess Press.
2. Love, Ann, and Jane Drake. 1999. *Kids and Grandparents: An Activity Book.* Niagara Falls, New York: Kids Can Press.
3. Rubin, Rhea Joyce. 1993. *Intergenerational Programming: A How-To-Do-It Manual for Librarians.* New York: Neal-Schuman.
4. Erickson, Lynne Martin, Rhea Rubin, and Maureen Wade, comp. "Services to the Elderly, List of One-Time Intergenerational Programs". American Library Association. www.ala.org/Content/ NavigationMenu/Our_Association/Offices/Literacy_and_Outreach_Se rvices/Outreach_Resources/List_of_Intergenerational_Programs.htm.

7

SURF THE NET WITH SENIORS

Learning is a treasure that will follow its owner everywhere.

—Chinese Proverb

OVERVIEW

Senior adults didn't grow up playing video games and using computers for everyday tasks, so they come to the library to see what all the "dot.com" fuss is about. Computers have become indispensable tools for researching information, keeping in touch with family and friends, and generally keeping up with changing times. According to Jupiter Research, the senior population online was estimated to be 4.4 million in 2001, and is expected to surge to 16.3 million by 2007. While statistics show and librarians can tell you that seniors love computers and are the fastest growing segment of the Internet community, some seniors have an initial fear of technology and are overwhelmed with all that computers and the Internet have to offer. When slowly introduced to the Internet, these same seniors are soon delighted to discover that they can use and benefit from this wealth of information.

This new medium is an advantage that offers many opportunities for seniors to expand their technological and general knowledge and confidence. Seniors will have access to beneficial information on health and fitness, retirement benefits, travel, and entertainment and will have an inexpensive way to communicate with faraway friends and relatives through e-mail and discussion groups. The Internet, with its dynamic and interactive means of communicating, playing, and shopping, allows seniors to stay connected, maintain relationships, and stimulate their minds—key factors in longevity. Online shopping can be more convenient for seniors who lack transportation or are homebound due to health

115

problems or disability, and surveys indicate that two-thirds of online shoppers are over forty.

A survey conducted by SeniorNet in 2002 indicated the following computer uses by seniors:

- 94% staying in touch with family and friends
- 70% researching health information
- 72% accessing news
- 52% making online purchases
- 38% playing games

COMPUTER TRAINING FOR SENIOR ADULTS

INTERNET ACCESS
REFERENCE DATABASES
THE LIBRARY WEB CATALOG

FRIDAY, DECEMBER 7TH
9:00 A.M. OR 11:00 A.M.

SPACE IS LIMITED!
CALL 622-0956 TO SIGN-UP!

Figure 7-1 Computer Training for Seniors Flyer

Another SeniorNet survey reported that seniors spend more time (twelve hours per week) at the computer than any other age group. Other popular computer activities included researching genealogy, producing memoirs, monitoring investments, and starting a business. In addition, seniors have created their own chat forums and write to their legislators via the Internet. Computer and Internet training is an important service that libraries can provide to seniors, allowing them to cross the "digital divide," thereby enriching their lives and promoting lifelong learning.

HOW SENIORS LEARN

In addition to learning *about* computers in introductory classes, seniors can explore learning *with the aid of* computers in more advanced classes that can teach them how to find distance learning opportunities and train them to use self-directed learning sites and CD-ROM software. Lifelong learning, an important component of well being, is available to all ages when travel and access are no longer barriers.

Research in the past several years has proven that age does not prevent us from learning new things, it only changes the way we learn. Older adults are more selective in what they choose to remember because many years of experience has taught them that they don't use everything they learn. In addition, older adults don't store general information as well as they store practical details, and performing new tasks requires more of their attention.

These facts provide valuable clues for how we should teach seniors about computers. Hands-on training is a senior's best way to learn and retain new information, so each student should have their own computer for the lessons. Seniors will be evaluating the usefulness of the information you present to them, so show them things that produce immediate results. Keep lessons practical by showing all the tasks the user can perform with the computer, and give names to classes that make their value more apparent. Present new tasks one step at a time, making sure they have time to practice and understand that step before going on so they may build on what they have learned. Explain unfamiliar terms and don't use technical jargon; relate the Internet to everyday things seniors know well by comparing Internet addresses to home addresses to demonstrate how each address is unique. Adopting the attitude of sharing information with an adult rather than teaching a child can help the adult student feel comfortable in the learning environment and reduce fear of failure.

The physical environment needs to be comfortable for a good learning experience. Ergonomic chairs and large screen monitors that allow screen space for larger font sizes are most helpful. Font size can be adjusted easily in an IE browser by clicking on "View" and "Text Size" and choosing the most comfortable size. Adjusting the height of the monitors by setting them on a base (a large book or two will work) may help bifocal wearers. Check the resources for vendors of large print peel-and-stick key tops that make the keys on the keyboard more visible to vision impaired users and other assistive technology for users who have vision loss. See Chapter 2 for several options for screen magnifiers and screen readers.

CLASS GUIDE

Our basic class form for adult learners is adapted from *Teaching Technology: a How-To-Do-It Manual for Librarians* by D. Scott Brandt:

- Get your students' attention by showing how they can use what they are going to learn. They will immediately see the usefulness of the information.

- Explain the goals and objectives of the lesson you will be showing them.

- Review any previous sessions and connect them to the new lesson. This step helps students build on skills they already know.

- Present the new lesson with lecture and demonstration in twenty minute (or less) units and recap. Encourage the students to take notes.

- Allow time for students to try the new knowledge and practice the process until they are comfortable with it.

- Give the students an exercise to demonstrate their new knowledge.

- Give feedback on their work through praise or encouragement.

- Evaluate whether they have reached the goals. A short quiz before and after the lesson will show you that your lessons are effective and give the students confidence that they have learned something new.

- Assign homework for additional reinforcement. Senior students need to repeat activities to develop new skills.

Following this basic guide, we can teach adult students everything they want to learn about the computer one step at a time. Make handouts in large print (at least fourteen point) for each lesson: a glossary of computer terms and simple definitions and/or illustrations, FAQ answers, step by step instructions, and resources, with space for notes. Some libraries adapt an online course to teach their students. Several sites with online courses are listed in the self-directed learning section. Give a few tips on Internet safety and explain your library's Internet policy. If you are creating your own beginner classes, here is a list of topics you will want to cover following the basic lesson guide for each step:

- Parts of the computer: Explain the visible parts of the computer, introducing and explaining new terms so the words become familiar—monitor, keyboard, mouse, hard drive, PC, CD drive, A drive, and browser are all terms beginners need to know and understand. Skip the internal parts for beginners.

- The Mouse: The mouse can be a hurdle for first time computer users, so slow down the mouse speed in the Control Panel to make the learning process less frustrating. Practicing hand/eye coordination is an important step for mastering the mouse, so make the practice time enjoyable by showing the seniors Solitaire games or by visiting www.ckls.org/~crippel/computerlab/tutorials/mouse/page1.html for online mouse practice.

- The Browser: The browser is the window to the Internet, and students will need to know a few of the basic browser tools to get started—the Forward and Back buttons, the Location or Address bar, the Home button for when they get lost, scroll bars, and arrow keys.

- The Internet: Explain that the Internet is a network of computers that all have unique addresses just like their own homes, and demonstrate that the parts of a Web address are unique like the components of their home postal address. The first part shows the type of transfer for that address, the second part is the address of the server or computer where the information is stored, and the domain extensions .com, .gov, and .org gives information about the organization that owns the site. Point out the address in the location box at each site they visit during the class.

- Visit Web sites: Show some Web addresses in magazines and books, pointing out there are no spaces and the importance of writing down addresses accurately from the television. Show them how to type in an address right in the address bar and using the "File" and "Open" menu option.

- Links: Explain that Web pages are connected through links and another site can be reached by merely clicking on a link. Point out how the mouse pointer turns into a hand when it discovers a link and that most links are a different color and/or underlined. Remind them of the Back and Forward buttons when they explore links.

- Search the Internet: Explain search engines, databases, and directories as three ways to search for information and to find sites when you do not know the address. Match the question to the tool when deciding which search engine to use. Google (www.google.com) is a good search engine to experiment with to learn the value of limiting the number of hits by adding terms or getting more hits by using fewer and more general terms. Avoid teaching all the features of a particular searching tool since they change frequently and this can be too much for beginners to remember. Show Yahoo's home page to explain a directory, and show one of your library's databases to show how they are different from a search engine.

- Bookmark favorites: Explain how to save favorite sites by making bookmarks in the browser.

ADVANCED CLASS NOTES

More advanced classes can be added when the students have mastered the basics—and the students will often tell the instructor what they want to learn next! Ongoing Beginner, Intermediate and Advanced classes or a periodic series of classes may work well in your library. Topics for Intermediate and Advanced classes that are helpful and interesting to seniors include (in no particular order):

- Improve searching skills; introduce more favorite search engines and teach seniors how to use directories.

- Introduce databases that are available at your library, including phone directories and periodical databases.

- Show how to register for an online e-mail account and use e-mail. Let the students experiment by e-mailing each other or one of the librarians on duty; an immediate reply is very gratifying and reinforces the lesson. Make the lesson fun by explaining emoticons, electronic greeting cards, and netiquette.

- Demonstrate how to save information on floppy disks and CDs.

- Teach seniors to evaluate Web sites and to determine if a Web site is trustworthy by asking who, what, when, where, why, and how. Who is the author of the site? What kind of information are you getting? When was the site created? Where is the site (look at the URL)? Why are you at this site, and is there a better place to get the information? How can you tell if the site is valid?

- Offer a tutorial on CD-ROM software.

- Explain how to use the programs available on the library computers, including word processors, PowerPoint, and spread sheets.

- Discuss how to shop safely online and how to protect your privacy.

- Show how to book hotel rooms, buy airline tickets, and make travel plans online.

- Discuss computer anatomy, for the truly curious!

- Talk about digital photography and discuss how to send photo files via e-mail. Demonstrate projects with digital photos like making iron-ons.

- Show how to use scanners to turn paper into digital files.

- Discuss how to buy a computer and invite a local computer sales representative to explain what features to look for and to explain the jargon computer sales people use.

- Teach seniors how to create a personal Web page at a free hosting site like Geocities.

- Explore the library's Web site and teach seniors to use the catalog, place holds, and check patron records from a remote location.

- Demonstrate popular software like Family Tree Maker or greeting card programs.

SELF-DIRECTED LEARNING

Seniors that seem able and anxious to continue their learning on their own and have computers at home can be directed to online computer instruction sites. The Internet is perfect for self-paced learning. Direct self-learners to a couple of these resources:

- AARP's Computer How To Guides (www.aarp.org/computers-howto/) are specialized lessons on specific computer related questions.

- Computers Made Easy (for senior citizens) (www.csuchico.edu/%7Ecsu/seniors/computing2.html#1.%20training) is a nonprofit Web site designed to help older adults understand how computers work and how to locate resources. It includes links to tutorial Internet sites as well as links to several senior organizations.

- SeniorNet (www.seniornet.org) is a nonprofit organization of computer-using adults age fifty and older with a mission to provide access and to educate other older adults about computer technologies. The site has over 220 Learning Centers, including tutorials for searching the World Wide Web, reader's guides, book discussions, a guide to using eBay, online courses, and e-greetings.

- Cyber Seniors (www.multcolib.org/seniors/index .html) is a page of tutorials offered by Multnomah County Public Library.

- Learn the Net (www.learnthenet.com/english/index.html) is a privately held company based in San Francisco offering step by step instructions on how to use the site, user friendly Internet training information on selected topics, and online courses for a minimal fee.
- The University of Missouri Outreach and Extension (www.outreach.missouri.edu/imaster) offers Internet training resources and guidelines for specific software programs such as WordPerfect.

Figure 7-2 Flyers are inexpensive ways to promote new services at the library.

Generations on Line
For Senior Adults

Internet access with step-by-step instructions
Simple to Understand
Friendly
Fast

*Now available for our senior patrons
at the Coshocton Public Library*

Includes e-mail
Access to the World Wide Web
Sites of special interest
Discussion board for sharing knowledge and
experiences with school children.

*This program was made available for the
Coshocton Public Library
by the William and Mary Ehrich Fund*

- *ComputerEase: A Beginner's Guide to Personal Computing* by Ellen Sue Spicer will help the self-directed learner and also give trainers tips on explaining the computer to seniors. Published in 2000 by Ground Hog Press, this guide is an easy-to-follow manual written by a senior adult. Call 877–337–2292 toll-free to order.

- *Generations on Line (GoL)* is a nonprofit computer program that can be purchased for use in the library for a one time fee of $250.00 per building. It includes larger print step-by-step instructions on using the Internet and e-mail using familiar terms, offers guidance in searching the Internet, and provides a series of popular links. A discussion board is available at GoL that enables classrooms of elementary children to post questions about the past that older adults can answer. See the resources for ordering information.

TUTORING PROGRAMS

Many libraries utilize volunteers for teaching computer classes and as coaches during classes. Peer volunteer coaches are usually less intimidating to seniors and can point out the practical application of the lessons from experience; however many other libraries have had success teaming up teens and seniors for computer tutoring sessions. Train the teens to work with older adults, making them aware of the different ways they learn and reminding them to be patient. Teach them the basic class form for teaching adults. Building cross-generation relationships is a side benefit for both age groups.

OFFSITE COMPUTER LESSONS

Some library systems are placing computers in the senior facilities in their communities or are collaborating with senior centers by offering teachers and volunteers to teach series of classes for their own computer labs.

Another option is a portable computer lab consisting of laptop computers with wireless cards that can be taken into the community to senior centers, nursing homes, assisted living facilities, and senior apartment complexes for lessons. Some residents only want a demonstration so they can see what the Internet is. ALA's Library Service and Technology Act offers mini grant opportunities for outreach services to introduce computers to seniors who are unable to come to the library themselves.

A Mobile Lab may be available to you for free. For example, the State Library of Ohio and Ohio Public Library Information Network (OPLIN) sponsor a Mobile Internet Training Lab—a retrofitted bookmobile equipped with eight computers and a networked printer—that can be reserved by any public library. A wireless Internet bridge connects to the library's router. Free delivery, pick-up, and help with setup is available to any public library in Ohio by calling 740–783–4385. Contact your state library to see if a similar program is available to your library.

COMPUTER CLUBS AND DISCUSSION LISTS

Form a computer club for seniors who have attended your classes so they can continue learning about computers and the Internet. Each meeting can focus on a specific topic the participants choose, and you can create a discussion list allowing seniors to sign up, discuss senior issues, ask computer questions, and build a network of local friends. Encourage social interaction among the students. Try an all day workshop; give a lesson in the morning, let the seniors have lunch together, and reconvene for practice in the afternoon. Programs like these build community.

SITES SENIORS LIKE

Many of these sites are frequented and enjoyed by seniors and provide needed information and entertainment. An annotated handout of sites to explore will help new users get an idea of all the possibilities the Internet offers.

- Game sites like http://games.yahoo.com, www.up roar.com, and www.pogo.com, along with any other casino, board, and word games are favorites that stimulate the mind and allow seniors to meet other players for social interaction.

- Shopping and auction sites such as www.ebay.com, www.qvc.com, and www.amazon.com are fun for "Windows Shopping" and browsing!

- Medical sites like www.webmd.com and www.nlm .nih.gov/medlineplus explain medical terms, conditions, and drug information in layman's terms.

- Medicare's site is available at www.medicare.gov.

- The Social Security site can be found at www.ssa.gov.

- FirstGov for Seniors (www.seniors.gov) has government information about benefits, health and nutrition, consumer protection, employment and volunteer activities, travel, education, and taxes.

- Your state government's Web site is a helpful link to include.

- Elderhostel (www.elderhostel.org) is a nonprofit organization that provides educational adventures for adults fifty-five and older.

- The AARP (www.aarp.com) has information for everyone aged fifty and older.

- The Alliance for Retired Americans (www.retired americans.org) is a new national organization that works to protect the health and economic security of seniors, rewards work, strengthen families and builds thriving communities.

- ElderNet (www.eldernet.com) is a user-friendly seniors' guide to health, housing, legal issues, finances, retirement, lifestyle, news, and information on the World Wide Web.

- 4Seniors.com (www.4seniors.4anything.com) offers links to shopping, health and fitness, travel and retirement planning sites.

- Senior Navigator (www.seniornavigator.com) provides free information about health and aging resources for Virginians. It also provides this information for seniors without access to computers through volunteer-staffed Senior Navigator Centers.

- Web Pointer for Senior Adults (http://web.pdx.edu/ ~psu01435/startup.html), developed by an older Oregon couple, includes lots of links that are helpful and interesting to seniors and is an inspiration to senior computer students who want to develop a Web page of their own.

- Senior Sites on the Web (www.ala.org/Content/ NavigationMenu/RUSA/Our_Association2/RUSA_ Sections/MOUSS/Our_Section4/Committees10/Lib rary_Services_to_an_Aging_Population/Sites_for_ Seniors.htm) is the American Library Association's list of sites for seniors.
- Cyndi's List of Genealogy Sites on the Internet can be found at www.cyndislist.com.
- Wired Seniors (www.wiredseniors.com/ageofrea son/) lists sites for the over-fifty crowd.
- RxList (www.rxlist.com) is an Internet drug index.
- SeniorLaw (www.seniorlaw.com) includes information about Elder Law, Medicare, Medicaid, estate planning, trusts, and the rights of the elderly and disabled.
- The National Senior Citizens Law Center is available at www.nsclc.org.

RESOURCES

1. Brandt, Scott D. 2002. *Teaching Technology: A How-To-Do-It Manual for Librarians*. New York: Neal-Schuman.

2. Lamdin, Lois, with Mary Fugate. 1997. *"Computers as Learning Tools," Elderlearning: New Frontier in an Aging Society.* Phoenix: Oryx Press, 132–136.

3. Medicare Information, An Easy Internet Lesson for People with Medicare. 2002. Ohio Department of Insurance and OSHIIP. Can be obtained by request: 1–800–686–1578.

4. Bradfield, Chris, and Jeanne Holba Puaez. 2000. "Surf's Up for Seniors! Introducing Older Patrons to the Web" *Computers in Libraries*, September.

5 Burwell, Lisa. 2001. "Too Old to Surf? No Way! An Internet Course for Seniors." *American Libraries*, November: 40–42.

6. Cohen, Laura B. 2001. "Ten Tips for Teaching How to Search the Web." *American Libraries*, November: 44–46.

7. Van Fleet, Connie, and Karen E. Antell. 2002. "Creating CyberSeniors: Older Adult Learning and Its Implications for Computer Training." *Public Libraries*, May/June:149–155.

8. Don Johnston Incorporated. "Keytop Overlays." www.tire sias.org/ equipment/keytop_overlays_labelling.htm.

9. MOUSS: American Library Association. "Senior Sites on the Web." www.ala.org/Content/NavigationMenu/RUSA/Our_Asso ciation2/RUSA_Sections/MOUSS/Our_Section4/Committees10/Libra ry_Services_to_an_Aging_Population/Sites_for_Seniors.htm.

10. Greenspan, Robyn. "Surfing with Seniors and Boomers." www.cyberatlas.internet.com/big_picture/demographics/arti cle/0,,5901_1573621,00.html.

11. "Too Old for Computers?" http://web.pdx.edu/~psu01435/ tooold.html.

12. SeniorNet Survey on Internet Use, November 2002. www.sen iornet.org/php/default.php?PageID=6880&Version=0&Font=0.

8 GROOM GREAT VOLUNTEERS

Act as if what you do makes a difference. It does.

—William James

OVERVIEW

Volunteers are good PR for libraries; a volunteer speaks for an organization without being paid to do so and the organization's service and support is more credible to patrons, who will see the volunteer as someone who is there because he or she wants to be. Volunteers are important because they can provide and expand services professionals cannot achieve due to limited time and full schedules. Volunteering is good for seniors, too. The senior volunteer contributes to the community and that contribution fortifies his or her feelings of self-worth. Libraries may train individuals, partner with a volunteer organization, host a Friends of the Library group, or develop a Senior Advisory Board to meet their need for volunteers. Freemont Public Library has a Web page (www.fremontlibrary.org/volunteers.asp) explaining their volunteer program that can help you develop one for your own library.

VOLUNTEER RECRUITMENT AND TRAINING

Libraries can recruit good volunteers through several avenues. A volunteer service may be available in the community that can help match jobs to people or notices in library newsletters and church bulletins can reach potential volunteers. Send position announcements to civic clubs and organizations, and encourage current volunteers to recruit friends who would like to volunteer.

Volunteers need to be acceptable to the library and also the institution where they will be serving if they will be working in an outreach program. Volunteers should fill out applications similar to an employee application and should be interviewed to determine their capabilities and motivations, how much time they can give, and when they are available. Not every person who volunteers will be a perfect match for library service, and it is best if the interview process can help the volunteer and the library find this out. Volunteers should:

- be people oriented
- be empathetic
- have an available car
- hold a valid driver's license
- have the physical stamina to carry a bag of books
- be dependable
- be stable
- have integrity
- be good listeners
- be accommodating.

Once volunteers are accepted, they need to be trained to represent the library in the community. An orientation including a review of library policies, a tour of the library, and an introduction to the staff they will work with, along with an assigned space, will make them feel a part of the organization. For each position, write a job description so there is a clear understanding of expectations and a basis for evaluation. Train the volunteers to do any needed library procedures; explain how they will report their work and who their supervisor is if they need information or help. Volunteers should be supervised by library staff and often work well in pairs.

JOBS FOR VOLUNTEERS

Library volunteers can complete jobs that library staff often have a hard time getting done—light cleaning, dusting shelves, or cleaning children's toys and equipment. They can help make programs special by preparing and serving refreshments. Children's departments need volunteers to help prepare craft materials, and the volunteers may like to help at story times and craft programs. Trained volunteer tutors can work with adult learners in literacy programs and listen to beginning young readers.

Senior volunteers can take library service out into the community by conducting read-aloud story times in preschools and elementary grade schools and providing homebound delivery service which might be impossible otherwise. The volunteers may be able to spend a little more time visiting with the residents and learn more about their preferences and relay that information to the librarian choosing materials. Trained as coaches, seniors can help individuals in computer and Internet classes or be paired up with a young student as a tutor.

SENIOR ADVISORY BOARD

Like a Teen Advisory Board, a Senior Advisory Board can serve several roles. Besides being a ready supply of trained volunteers, they can also help develop programs and be spokesmen for the library in the community. Applications, orientation, and training will make this group indispensable. Hold monthly meetings to encourage the members to develop working relationships that lead to brainstorming sessions, new friendships, and productive work teams.

FRIENDS OF THE LIBRARY

The Friends of the Library is a national group of volunteer library supporters. While Friends groups are not limited to senior adult membership, it is often the retired seniors who have the time and interest to contribute to the library. A Friends group can be a valuable asset to a library, generating funds for programming and special items that no longer fit into ever-tightening library budgets by, for example, operating bookstores that sell discarded and donated books to the public.

ESTABLISHING A FRIENDS GROUP

The *Friends of Libraries Sourcebook* is an invaluable resource for establishing a Friends group in your library. From getting organized to fundraising and developing literary landmarks, the Sourcebook has work sheets to help you; experiences and programs from many libraries are included as models. The Friends of Libraries Web site (www.folusa.org) gives many tips for starting a group and ideas for

Figure 8-1 You can't take the librarian out of the library! Grace Agricola, eighty, became a Friend of the Library twelve years ago when she retired from Coshocton Public Library as a children's librarian. She uses her cataloguing skills to sort the donations for the Friend's Books Galore book store.

services and fundraising. Friends organizations for each state are listed at www.folusa.org/html/statefol.html, and the instructions for joining an electronic discussion list for Friends to share ideas and information is included in the resources at the end of the chapter.

Figure 8-2: Friends of the Library Application

An Invitation to Join
the Friends Of the Library

If you are already a Friend, it's time to renew!

Recognizing the value of libraries to local communities as well as to humanity as a whole, the Coshocton Friends of the Library was founded in 1993 to enhance library services, provide community interaction with library operations as well as staff, and to create public awareness of the wealth of knowledge that libraries contain.

What do friends do?

Some Friends volunteer at the Books Galore Book Store, either as cashiers or as book sorters. Other Friends pitch in and help with the big once-a-year Book Sale. In May and June the Friends help prepare for the Summer Reading Program. A handful of Friends serve as hostesses for the Senior Tea Parties. Friends who like to cook prepare breakfast for the Library staff every Valentine's Day. Lots of Friends attend meetings the 2nd Wednesday of each month at 12:00 noon in the Large Meeting Room to help dream up new programs like Books for Babies and ways to raise money for the Library. Some Friends simply pay their dues each year. All Friends help make things happen at the Library!

How Do Friends' Contributions help the Library ?

The Friends support the work of the library by providing funds for:

Speakers Fees
Refreshments for Children, Teen, and Adult Programs
Special equipment for the Library
And Much More!

You are invited to join the Friends!
Complete the form Below:

Name_____

Address_____

Phone_____

Membership: Please check one ___$10.00 Member ___$25.00 Patron
                                              ___$25.00 Family   ___$50.00 Sustaining

Volunteer Opportunities:
___children's programs   ___working at book sale (once or twice a year)   ___attending meetings
___sorting books   ___working at Books Galore   ___ other

Signature_____Date_____

Please make checks payable to Friends of the Library.
Send to 655 Main St., Coshocton, OH 43812
Membership year July 1, 2002 – June 30, 2003.

FINDING PROJECTS

"Books for Babies" is a literacy program many Friends groups provide through hospitals to parents of newborns. A first book for the baby is presented with a packet explaining the importance of reading to your child to develop language skills. More special projects accomplished by Friends groups are described at www.folusa.org/html/best4.html, including publications, fund-raisers, and programs.

VOLUNTEER APPRECIATION

Just like paid employees, volunteers need a sense of job satisfaction. Keep good volunteers by telling them they are appreciated, giving specific examples when possible. Listen to their concerns and observations, give them as many staff privileges as possible (such as no fines and access to the staff room for break time), and recognize them periodically with a formal ceremony or special event. A luncheon catered by a grateful library staff is an inexpensive and fun event that will show true appreciation to your volunteers.

RESOURCES

1. Casey, Genevieve M. 1984. *Library Services for the Aging.* Hamden, CT: Library Professional Publications.

2. Dobelstein, Andrew W., with Ann B. Johnson. 1985. *Serving Older Adults: Policy, Programs, and Professional Activities.* Englewood Cliffs, NJ: Prentice-Hall.

3. Dolnick, Sandy, ed. 1996. *Friends of Libraries Sourcebook, 3rd ed.* Chicago: American Library Association.

4. "Friends of Libraries, U.S.A." www.folusa.org.

5. Fremont Public Library District. "Volunteer Services and Opportunities." www.fremontlibrary.org/volunteers.asp.

6. Friends of Libraries Discussion Group. Send an e-mail message to listproc@galegroup.com, leaving the subject line blank. In the body of the message, type only: subscribe FOLUSA-L, followed by your name.

PART II: HOW TO DELIVER LIBRARY SERVICES TO SENIORS WHERE THEY LIVE

9 TAKE THE LIBRARY TO THE HOMEBOUND

Reading—the best state yet to keep absolute loneliness at bay.

—William Styron

OVERVIEW

Being a lifelong reader myself, I don't know what I would do without books! You can take the library to the lifelong readers in your community when they are no longer able to come to you. Whether at home for the long-term due to physical limitations or for a short-term recovery period after surgery or illness, homebound patrons appreciate having library materials available to them. Reading brings information, news, recreation, and enjoyment that helps dispel the loneliness and depression that can come from being homebound.

Providing homebound service is excellent PR for the library as the community sees the library meeting the needs of all of its citizens. This service can become so important in an older person's life that they leave bequests to the library in thanks. Small or large, many libraries across the country see the importance of this service to their senior patrons and are delivering thousands of books and other materials every day.

A sample of a library policy covering homebound service is included in this chapter as a model for determining your own library's own policy. A policy, mission statement, or statement of philosophy should explain the library's goals for this service, define the target audience, and list the eligibility criteria. A definition of eligibility may be helpful in determining who qualifies for this service in your community. Many libraries require an application signed by a medical professional, while some libraries are comfortable with determining eligibility by evaluating individual circumstances or providing service to anyone who requests it. Tips for publicity, applications, readers advisory, keeping

Figure 9-1 Display flyers promoting the homebound service at the library, senior centers, doctors' offices and hospital waiting rooms.

**The Coshocton Public Library
Makes House Calls!**

The library offers free delivery to all residents of Coshocton County who are disabled or homebound because of long-term illness or advanced age and are physically unable to come to the library.

We deliver books, magazines, large print, audio and video materials. Call 622-0956 and ask for Sara or Pam to schedule for monthly deliveries.

patron logs, using volunteers, and organizing the service are also addressed.

SAMPLE HOMEBOUND SERVICE POLICY

Holmes County District Public Library

Statement of Philosophy for Outreach Services

The Holmes County District Public Library is committed to providing library materials and information to all residents of its service area. Delivery of library materials to residents who are unable to visit a fixed facility due to illness, disability, lack of transportation, or care-giving to a person needing continuous care is part of the commitment. Library staff members provide delivery service on a four to six week schedule.

Figure 9-2 Publicize the homebound service with a display case that will remind patrons of family and friends who would benefit from home delivery of library materials.

Residents receive materials on a regularly scheduled basis. Homebound service may be discontinued or modified for safety reasons. Service may also be discontinued if the purpose for the service is not being met.

Eligibility for Outreach Services Policy

To be eligible for home delivery of library materials, a patron must:

1. Reside in Holmes County
2. Be unable to get to a fixed library facility due to health or lack of transportation
3. Be a caregiver to a person requiring continuous care

Service is either temporary or permanent depending on patron wishes.

Institutions and senior centers within the county boundaries are eligible to receive delivery of library materials. Institutions include, but are not limited to, nursing homes, senior centers, hospitals, correctional facilities, and assisted living centers.

Figure 9-3 A homebound patron eagerly looks over the new library materials she has just received.

PUBLICITY

Since the homebound patrons are not frequenting the library, reaching them with the news of this service becomes the first task. Flyers at the main desk of the library and at senior community centers will catch the

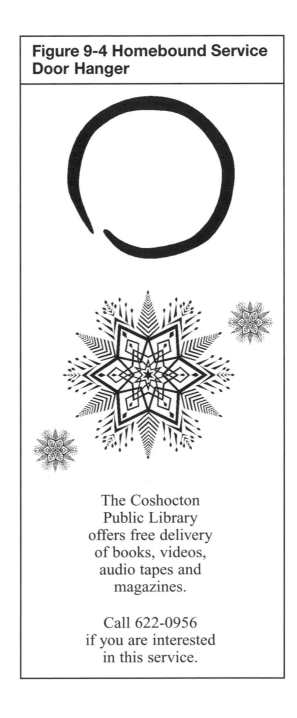

Figure 9-4 Homebound Service Door Hanger

The Coshocton
Public Library
offers free delivery
of books, videos,
audio tapes and
magazines.

Call 622-0956
if you are interested
in this service.

Figure 9-5 Homeword Bound Bookmark

eyes of patrons who have a relative or neighbor in need of the service. Placing the flyers in doctors' offices, senior community centers, and hospital waiting rooms will connect with more patrons needing the service for a short-term or long-term basis. Meals on Wheels or other meal delivery organization may deliver flyers directly to clients, and church and synagogue members who visit the homebound may be willing to deliver information to them. Senior Fairs are an excellent opportunity to publicize homebound and other library services for seniors.

Radio and newspaper ads will also reach many homebound patrons. Door hangers that advertise the service can be distributed a few times a year in assisted living residences. Activity directors can direct you to their residents that would benefit from personal book delivery service to their rooms or apartments. An explanation of the homebound delivery service, eligibility, and contact information should also be on the library's Web site, and an online application form is an added convenience.

Print publicity flyers on light paper with large type in dark ink to explain the basics of the program. Include the phone number to apply for the service and the Web site address if applications or more information is available online and list the eligibility requirements and what materials are available for delivery. Clearly state that this service is free, since many older patrons are living on fixed incomes and cost would be a major concern.

PATRON APPLICATIONS

Online or paper application forms will begin the process of getting to know your homebound patrons. If a doctor's signature is required by the library's administration, state it clearly on the application form and include space for the signature. The application and an interview will help the librarian determine what materials the library may have that will meet the patron's needs. The interview can be done over the telephone or during a first visit if the patron has difficulty using a phone.

Figure 9-6 A profile for each Homebound Patron will help with readers advisory.

Homebound Patron Profile

Name _____ Library card # _____

Address _____

Phone _____ In an emergency contact _____

Reason for service _____

Delivery person _____

Delivery instructions _____

Delivery schedule _____

Number of items per visit _____

Preferred Format: Large Print   Audio   Video   Paperback

Genre Preferences:

Western   Romance   Mystery   Historical   Adventure   Fantasy   Contemporary
Best Sellers   Gothic   Inspirational   Other _____

Biography   Travel   History   Nature/Animals   Science   Humor   Sports
Cooking   Crafts   Other_____

Hobbies and special interests: _____

Record all contact information, establish a delivery schedule, and collect any additional information that is required for library card application. Ask about any special instructions for delivery, including which door to go to, if there are pets that will greet the delivery person at the door, and if a phone call is necessary before delivery. Homebound patrons will feel more secure if the visits are prearranged. Give the patron your business card or make a large print bookmark with your contact information on it so they may call and request materials. Keep the applications and interviews on file to consult when collecting materials for the patrons and when making visits. Check out these online application forms for ideas for composing your own:

- Brampton Public Library's Special Needs/Services (www.bramlib.on.ca/special_services.htm)
- Spartanburg County Public Libraries (www.spt.lib. sc.us/homebnd.htm)
- Greendale Public Library (www.greendale.org/ library/l-homebound.html)
- Saline County Library (www.saline.lib.ar.us/tem plates/hb_ap.html)

READER'S ADVISORY

You are the patron's eyes and ears at the library, choosing the materials they will enjoy, so an interview is necessary to start learning about their reading interests. On a separate sheet or on the application, record answers to the following questions and any other helpful notes:

- What is the preferred format?
- Do you mostly read fiction or nonfiction?
- What are your favorite fiction genres?
- What are your favorite nonfiction subject areas?
- What are your hobbies or special interests?
- Do you have a career field you want to keep up with?
- Do you have any guidelines regarding sex, violence, or strong language?
- How many items would you like each month?

The first visits will be an experimental adjustment period as the visiting librarian refines the interview information to learn the patron's taste in reading material. Continue adding notes to the interview sheets that will help you select materials. One of my former patrons requested thin, paperback, historical European romances, with no sex or strong language, not written in the first person. It took a few visits to hit exactly what she was looking for, as she added a new restriction with each visit! I finally found books she loved: regency romances, except the ones written in first person. Format and genre are important as well as language and content. Often the weight of a book is a consideration because large print titles can be much heavier than their regular-print counterparts. After you get to know the patron, you might suggest new and different genres to broaden their reading interests.

Take library newsletters, booklists, and review publications like *BookPages* to your patrons so they can see what new books are arriving at the library. Book club ads in magazines are great for homebound patrons to browse for titles, and they may also enjoy books they hear about on television or NPR. Hennepin County Public Library publishes its own newsletter to keep homebound patrons up to date with new books. Ravenous Readers eNews is available online at www.hclib.org/pub/books/ravenousreaders.cfm. Become a great reader's advisor by becoming familiar with read-alikes, different genres, authors, award winners, and various series. Attend reader's advisory workshops whenever possible, and read or listen to books from genres that aren't familiar to you. Learn how to scan a book in five minutes to determine content and style, watch movies based on novels, and check the resources at the end of this chapter for materials to develop your skills. Soon you will be looking at new books and immediately thinking of one of your patrons who would like it.

The number of items you take each time will vary depending upon the patron's reading appetite and the duration between visits. One visit each month or every six weeks seems to work best for many libraries and their patrons. Libraries that serve the homebound on an as-needed basis have found that requests pick up when patrons are called periodically or when a publicity push has been done at a senior fair or other event.

PATRON LOGS

Several automated circulation systems, such as Dynix or Workflows, have a homebound service module that can record materials when checked out, print out a delivery receipt with a rating form attached, and prompt a rating for each item when it is checked in. The records accumulate in the computer, and a printed alphabetical record of this

Figure 9-7 Label shelves for each patron where materials can be collected for delivery.

information can be generated periodically to keep in a notebook with the patron interview. The librarian can take the patron log notebook to the shelves with a book cart and select materials for several patrons at once. To activate these features, change the patron type to "homebound," add a "no fine" status, and have overdue notices sent to the outreach staff rather than the patron. Homebound modules may have additional features that make paper records unnecessary by allowing all of the pertinent selection tips and delivery information recorded in the interviews to be added to each patron's record.

Libraries that do not have automated homebound modules will need to keep records manually. Index card files or lists typed in a word processing program are two options that have been used successfully. When a patron has read a title, the index card can be filed alphabetically by author and kept in small file boxes or in file drawers from an old card catalog—whatever is convenient to carry to the shelves. A series name or books by a favorite author can be recorded on the same card. Lists typed in a word processor can be kept in a notebook like the computer printouts, and the file can be updated as needed. A temporary method that has been tried in some libraries is marking the materials with the patron's initials, but this system becomes problematic with different formats and when there are patrons with the same initials. However, for a small collection and a small homebound patron audience, this system is workable and inexpensive.

After the books are collected on the cart, they are checked out to the homebound department and arranged on shelves labeled with the patrons' names for each day of deliveries. Bookmarks, publications, new book lists, and library newsletters can be added to each stack, ready for delivery.

DELIVERIES

While a library staff member should oversee the organization of this service and conduct initial interviews, many people can be trained to help with the delivery and pickup process. For example, deliveries can be scheduled around the bookmobile's routes throughout the county or city. In areas inaccessible or not served by the bookmobile, deliveries can be made by outreach staff or trained volunteers.

As described in the Partnership chapter, a library found a practical, inexpensive way to provide homebound service by partnering with Meals on Wheels. Their trained volunteers are now serving up books as well as meals, and the library is reaching many more patrons. Members of the library staff may be willing to drop books off on their way home from work, or members of the patron's family may be able to deliver items, but need the librarian to choose the materials and keep records. Ask the Friends of the Library or the Teen Advisory Board to make homebound deliveries as a service project or ask if visiting nurses would be willing to deliver library materials to their patients.

Each homebound patron should have the same one or two people delivering books, if possible. The consistency will add to their feelings of safety when answering the door and help establish a comfortable relationship with the library. An ideal arrangement for the first delivery would be for the librarian who conducted the initial interview to take the person who will be delivering the items to the patron's home and introduce them to each other. Library staff and volunteers need to read the interview carefully, be friendly and nonthreatening in appearance, and be dependable in making the regular visits. Book selection will become easier as the patron and library representative become acquainted, but when someone else is doing the delivery, the coordinator will need to call the patrons periodically to see if the library is sending items they like.

BOOKS-BY-MAIL

Books-By-Mail delivers books right to the patron's mailbox in durable bags with postage paid tags via the U.S.P.S. Patrons return materials by placing them in the same bag and putting them in their mailbox. Eligibility for the service and loan periods varies with each library system, but the U.S. Post Office has specific requirements for free deliveries. Patrons usually request books by phone from a catalog mailed to them or online from an online catalog. Some libraries use a Books-By-Mail service to supplement personal delivery service. Those who use it in place of personal deliveries save staff time because there is no needed contact with the patron, but the added benefits of human contact is lost. Calling the patrons periodically to offer readers advisory will generate more use of the service.

The Ohio Valley Area Libraries (OVAL) offers a Books-By-Mail catalog online (http://bbm.oval.lib.oh.us) where patrons can order materials to be delivered right to their mailboxes. The Muskingum County Public Library contracts with OVAL for the service for their patrons. The library mails the catalogs and OVAL takes care of filling the requests and mailing the books. The library serves 318 homebound patrons through OVAL at a cost of $400–$500 per month.

STATISTICS

Each month, record the number of patrons served, the number of home visits, and the number of items circulated, report your statistics to the library administration, and keep them for your own records. The statistics can support a request for additional help as the service grows and can show your program is well used if you want to apply for a grant or partner with another agency. When you speak at community meetings, include statistics and personal stories about this wonderful service. Record anecdotal comments by patrons and special stories for your own inspiration and for support. Personal stories are the most convincing reasons for establishing homebound service and will cultivate support from your community.

Figure 9-8 Here is a sample of a statistical report form for a Senior Services Department.

Outreach Statistics
_____ 2003

INDIVIDUAL SERVICE:

Patrons   ____
Visits   ____
Items Circulated   ____

INSTITUTIONS SERVED:

	Items	Visits	Programs	Attendance
Autumn Health Care Nursing	___	___	___	___
Jacob's Dwelling Nursing Center	___	___	___	___
Windsorwood Place	___	___	___	___
West Lafayette Care Center	___	___	___	___
Coshocton Care Center	___	___	___	___
Extended Care Facility	___	___	___	___
Riverside Tower	___	___	___	___
Coffee Club	___	___	___	___
Grand Time @ the Library	___	___	___	___
Special Programs	___	___	___	___
Totals	___	___	___	___

Total Items Circulated   _____

_____

Outreach Coordinator

RESOURCES

1. Saricks, Joyce G., and Nancy Brown. 1997. _Readers' Advisory Service in the Public Library_. Chicago: American Library Association.

2. Shearer, Kenneth D., and Robert Burgin, eds. 2001. _The Reader's Advisor's Companion_. Englewood, CO: Libraries Unlimited.

3. Strauss, Karen. 2003. "Your Books Are in the Mail: Launching a Books by Mail Program." _Public Libraries_ 42, no. 1 (January/February): 47–50.

4. Bookwire. "Book Awards." www.bookwire.com/bookwire/otherbooks/Book-Awards.html.

5. "Book Magazine." www.bookmagazine.com.

6. "Book Page: America's Book Review". www.bookpage.com.

7. Bookmarks Magazine. "For Everyone Who Hasn't Read Everything." www.bookmarksmagazine.com.

8. United States Postal Service. "Free Matter for the Blind and Other Physically Handicapped Persons." http://pe.usps.gov/cpim/ftp/manuals/dmm/E040.pdf.

9. Libraries Unlimited. "Genreflecting." www.genreflecting.com.

10. Hirsch, Jane K. "How to Read a Book in Five Minutes." South Jersey Regional Library Cooperative. www.sjrlc.org/RAhandouts/5minutes.htm.

11. American Library Association. "Libraries Providing Home Delivery Service: A Sampling of Active Programs." www.ala.org/Content/NavigationMenu/Our_Association/Offices/Literacy_and_Outreach_Services/Outreach_Resources/Libraries_Providing_Home-Delivery_Service__A_Sampling_of_Active_Programs.htm.

12. Morton Grove Public Library. "Webrary." www.webrary.org.

10 TAKE THE LIBRARY TO RESIDENTIAL FACILITIES

All of life is a constant education.

—Eleanor Roosevelt

OVERVIEW

Many older adults reside in assisted living residences or nursing homes for health and safety reasons. Those living with relatives may spend their days in adult day care programs while their families are at work, and others who can find transportation to nutritional centers or senior centers may spend their days there for some social activities and meals. Rehab hospitals and adult learning centers are also places to find groups of seniors in need of library services, yet unable to come to the library.

Initiate a library card drive targeting all the senior facilities in your community to empower this population with access to the library collection. Call the directors of these facilities, describe the services you are able to offer, discuss the options with them so they can decide which will work best for their residents, and perhaps suggest putting together an informal focus group of residents and activity directors to decide what materials would be most appreciated. Establish good working relationships with the directors and activity directors by being dependable and accessible so you are better able to serve their residents as patrons.

Bookmobiles have often stopped at these facilities, but the bookmobile steps can be a barrier to many of the residents. Some bookmobiles are equipped with wheelchair lifts, but a lot of shelving space is lost to make room for the mechanism, and the steps are still an obstacle for patrons with walkers. An ELF (extremely low floor) vehicle is more accessible, eliminating steps with a lower profile floor that allows patrons to walk right in or even roll in with a wheelchair. Using the

151

bookmobile or book van to make lobby stops or deliver deposit collections will make a collection more accessible to the residents.

Promote the library with displays, posters, and book talks or discussions at the facilities. You are taking the library to the patrons, so remember to take newsletters and other library publications with you, take the time to visit and offer readers advisory, and make sure they are aware of the various formats available to them.

LOBBY STOPS

In a "lobby stop," library staff take carts of books into the main gathering area of a facility for patrons to browse and check out. An ELF bookmobile's low profile makes using book carts for lobby stops even more convenient, and books can be checked out directly to patrons using their own cards with a laptop computer connected real time to the library's circulation system via an air card and cellular connection. If a cellular connection is not possible, a portable barcode reader (a Telxon, for example) can record the transactions so they may be loaded into the library's circulation system after returning to the library. Show seniors how to reserve their own materials in facilities that have Internet access, or place holds for them while you are there. Plan the stop for an hour and the bookmobile driver can make other scheduled stops in the neighborhood and come back to pick up the books, carts, and staff working at the facility.

DEPOSIT COLLECTIONS

A deposit collection is a small library collection checked out to a facility's institutional card for a period of time for their residents to use. Deposit collections can be used for homebound service or in libraries lacking enough staff members or a bookmobile. The deposits provide readers with a changing collection of library materials conveniently accessible to them. Activity directors can fax, call, or e-mail special requests to the library for the patrons or advise the librarian about what titles and formats are best for their residents.

The sizes of the collections vary from library to library, depending on the needs and population of the residence and the frequency with which the collection will be rotated. Collections as small as fifteen books to over 200 books were reported by libraries providing this service, with loan periods from one to three months. Deposit collections may be shelved in the facility's library or activity room, and may be wheeled around on a cart in nursing homes.

To establish deposit collections, ask the facility's director to write a letter on business letterhead addressed to the library's administrator requesting an institutional card, accepting financial responsibility for all items checked out on the card, and listing who may use the card. After the application is approved by the library administrator, a card is made and kept on file at the library with a list of the user names. The user list can also be added to the computer record of the account so any clerks asked to access the card record would immediately be aware of the approved users.

The outreach or bookmobile staff can then choose the materials from the collection, check them out to the card, and deliver them to the facility. Deliveries and pickup can be provided either by the library's courier service or the facility. The actual circulation is the responsibility of the activity director, who may choose to provide a notebook for residents to sign out books in the collection area, or in the case of a day care facility or nursing home, the patrons may sign out a book directly from the activity director. Sign-out cards may work in some residences and the library can also insert a card in each item for each reader to sign for their own records. While the items will show one circulation in the computer system from the initial checkout to the facility, circulation from the written records can be added to the statistics for a more accurate total. The written circulation records will also show what items are being read, which will help material selection for future deposit collections.

Set up a regular scheduled time for pick up and drop off of deposit collections so the activity director is able to collect the materials from the residents by the due date. A phone call reminder a few days ahead of time is a courtesy that will give residents time to finish the materials and the activity director time to collect them. Fines are usually waived for these collections, since the patron is dependent on others to get the book returned on time.

If there are several facilities to serve with deposit collections, divide the materials evenly into separate collections and rotate them among those facilities. The Friends of the Library may be interested in helping fund new additions to the deposit collection.

RESOURCES

FOR OVERVIEW

1. Farber Specialty Vehicles. "E.L.F." www.farberspecialty.com/ELF/ELF.htm.

11 TAKE YOUR PROGRAMS TO RESIDENTIAL FACILITIES

To improve the golden moment of opportunity, and catch the good that is within our reach, is the great art of life.

—Samuel Johnson

OVERVIEW

Activity directors of nursing homes and residential facilities are always looking for interesting programs and activities for their residents, and the library can provide several options for informative, entertaining, and educational programs for these patrons by offering programming materials and resources to activity directors, training volunteers to conduct programs, or conducting the programs yourself. Whoever provides programming for these facilities needs to be aware of what activities are already provided, be a good planner, and be comfortable conducting group activities.

Invite area nursing home and residential facility activity directors to a tea at the library, explain the options you are prepared to offer to them, and show them samples of program kits and a list of sample program themes you can present. Listen to their suggestions and let the activity directors determine which of the services will best serve their residents.

If the library staff or library volunteers will be providing programming, establish a regular schedule for visits and set guidelines for each facility. You might request that the residents be ready in the activity room at your arrival and a staff member be present during the program. Most programs should be limited to thirty to forty-five minutes to not overtire the residents. Maintain contact with the activity directors to be aware of changing resident interests and needs; initiate these calls as activity directors can be very busy.

155

Reach out to seniors living in senior apartment complexes and assisted living facilities by providing programming that introduces the library and its collection to nonusers and encourages reading and literacy. Send individual invitations to residents for special programs and arrange distribution through the apartment or facility office managers. Ask if you can submit publicity about programs if they have a newsletter, place posters on their bulletin boards or in the elevators to announce new services or programs, and use door hangers for announcements, invitations, and news.

Older adults have varied interests and experiences, so programs can take on many forms and cover a wide variety of topics. Programs presented at the library can often be adapted for use in outside facilities, so keep the different audiences in mind when planning. For example, active, independent seniors visiting senior centers or living in senior apartment complexes may be able to enjoy longer, more active programs that offer opportunities for participation, whereas elderly residents in nursing homes or in day care facilities may enjoy a lighter version of the same program and benefit from more personal interaction and sensory stimulation.

Books and other library materials related to the program topic should always be displayed and available for checkout to make a connection to the collection. Take props, and remember to speak clearly and slowly or use a microphone, and make large, colorful visual aids and large print handouts to make the programs more visually interesting. Children's books are useful for many of the programs because of the large colorful pictures and the condensed information.

Music and song are important elements in programming for the elderly. Christo Pantev, a neuroscientist and musician who has researched music and memory loss in the elderly for several years, found during his studies at Toronto's Rotman Research Institute that the last items to remain in the memories of his patients were music and songs. Offering melodies and lyrics from their youth will inspire memories as well as smiles from the elderly patrons.

The programs in this chapter have worked well in many types of senior facilities for librarians across the country. Ask your library volunteers and teen groups to help when you need props or crafts prepared ahead of time or assistance serving refreshments.

REMEMBERING PROGRAMS

Reminiscing is beneficial to the elderly and a normal and important part of growing older. Seniors participating in remembering programs are less withdrawn and apathetic, because reminiscing promotes mental and emotional well-being and combats isolation, loneliness, and depression by allowing seniors to connect with things that matter to them, the things that shaped their lives. Besides exercising the memory to help it to perform more efficiently, reminiscing can create a bond among program participants as they discover similar experiences and memories. Nursing home residents and adult day care patrons will benefit the most from these remembering programs.

PROGRAM KITS FOR REMEMBERING PROGRAMS

BiFolkal Kits are programming kits created to stimulate all five senses to trigger memories and discussion for older adults. A kit includes a manual, a slide carousel, story books, game sheets, songs, poems, realia objects, scratch and sniff cards, and audio tapes, all packaged in a tote. Library staff can visit facilities and present programs with these kits, and trained volunteers and activity directors can be taught how to utilize them to provide regular, enjoyable senior programming in their

Figure 11-1 Remembering School Days from BiFolkal Productions is a complete program kit for activity directors and busy librarians.

own facilities. The School Days, Aprons, Cars, Farms, and County Fairs kits are among seniors' favorites. Actiphiles, Program Manuals, and Slideas can be purchased separately from BiFolkal kits as a base for building your own programs. More information about BiFolkal and other programming kits can be found in Chapter 2.

You can combine library materials with a few props borrowed from home or coworkers to create your own program kits. Your kits should provide opportunities for one-on-one interaction with the audience as the props are shared. Keep in mind the concept of stimulating all five senses and involving the audience when compiling the materials for your nursing home program theme kits:

- Hearing: stories, poems, jokes, music, read-aloud, sing-along, audiotapes
- Seeing: pictures, photos, book displays, costumes, props
- Touching: items to pass around, hold, and touch
- Smelling: scented lotions, food, flowers, spices, flavorings, scratch and sniff cards
- Tasting: refreshments, snacks, favors
- Audience Participation: sing-along, trivia quizzes, puzzles, games, discussion

"My Favorite Books and Character Dolls" is a program kit you can make that combines favorite children's classics with character dolls. When promoting the program, ask the audience to bring a favorite book and/or character doll from a favorite book to share. Titles that seniors will remember from their childhoods are *Little Women, Pinocchio, Raggedy Ann and Andy, The Tale of Peter Rabbit, Wizard of Oz* and other children's classics. Adapt this program for an intergenerational audience by adding contemporary books and dolls.

ElderSong Publications, Inc. also sells prepared program kits such as *Yesterdays* by Nancy Dezan, a collection of twenty nostalgic read-aloud short stories with accompanying photograph plates, questions for discussion, fun facts, and trivia games. More information about ElderSong's programming materials is available in Chapter 2.

At $10.00, "Our Town" is an inexpensive, enjoyable remembering card game that can be used with nursing home residents or in an intergenerational setting to lead the players to share their life experiences. Check it out at www.missouri.edu/~projlife/ourtown.htm.

Inspire seniors to share their memories by using antique collections available to you or borrowed from friends or relatives to create more nostalgia programs. Do you have a friend or coworker that collects feed sacks, aprons, antique hats, school memorabilia, or old kitchen uten-sils? All of these items bring back fond memories as they are passed among the audience. Smiles and discussion will naturally result when you share books with pictures, information, and trivia about the collec-tions and the times they were used. The residents enjoy looking at the items, touching them, trying on items, guessing what the utensils were used for, and sharing the memories inspired by the experiences. Check the resources at the end of the chapter for library materials to use with the aprons and kitchen gadgets programs.

SPEAKERS AND AUDIO VISUAL PRESENTATIONS FOR REMEMBERING PROGRAMS

REMEMBER WHEN

Learn about your audience's special interests and heritage and hire paid guest speakers to present a "Remember When" remembering program series to entertain and enlighten seniors on topics such as WWII, pet therapy, and the Kinder transport from Germany in the 1930s. The library that contributed this idea also held a holiday concert by a local school's hand bell choir.

THEN AND NOW

Share local history photos and lead discussion for a thirty to forty-five minute "Then and Now" slide show program for audiences at senior facilities of all kinds. Scan the photos, load them into a PowerPoint pro-gram, add short captions to label them, and discuss related information about the sites. Old photos from the local history collection contrasted with current photos of the same views are interesting discussion-starters. Make notes of or record the recollections of the residents about the photos to add to the local history collection files. You can develop a series of programs, each focusing on a different type of building or area of the city: one room schools, old factories, courthouses around the state, parks, or covered bridges. Use the technology that is available to you; the same program can be done with an overhead projector if you print the photo files on transparencies with added captions.

OLD-TIME RADIO

"Golden Moments of Radio" provides topics for a whole series of programs featuring old-time detective, comedy, variety show, western, adventure, and science fiction radio serials. You can present the program yourself or invite retired radio personalities, old-time radio buffs, or a performing arts professor to speak. Play audio tapes of radio programs from the library collection or broadcasts downloaded from the Internet and demonstrate sound effects used in the radio programs for an additional activity. Books with photos of the actors and the history of radio and an antique radio are visual aids that will bring back fond memories. Try this program with an active audience at a senior center and recruit them to read a radio script readers-theatre style and to perform the sound effects!

SEASONAL PROGRAMS

A calendar is a good guide for holiday and seasonal program ideas to keep nursing home residents involved in the current happenings of the community, to celebrate the changing of the seasons, and to provide the opportunity to reminisce about the holidays of their younger years. Refreshments can be served to make the programs more festive. Our local nursing homes have advised that diets don't usually have to be observed for special events and small treats, but it is nice to provide sugarless alternatives. Check with the activity directors before providing refreshments, so no one will be disappointed. A puzzle, bookmark, craft, favor or other appropriate small handout gift will make your audience feel special and will be a remembrance of the program.

WINTER PROGRAMS

SNOW

How full of creative genius is the air in which these are generated! I should hardly admire them more if real stars fell and lodged on my coat.

—Henry David Thoreau

Snow, snowmen, and snowflakes make wintertime a wonderland. Ask residents how they spent their winters growing up. Did they enjoy making snow angels, snowmen, sledding, and ice skating, or just curling up with a blanket, a hot cup of tea or cocoa and a book? Set the mood for this program with the poem "Stopping By Woods on a Snowy Evening" by Robert Frost. Tell the story of Snowflake Bentley, the man who spent his life studying snowflakes, and show his photographs of ice crystals in his book *Snow Crystals*. Bring stuffed or ceramic snowmen for visual aids and demonstrate how to make paper snowflakes and ask if anyone would like to make one. Make "snowman soup" for a handout at the end of the program: scoop instant hot cocoa mix into a small plastic bag tied with a ribbon and add a peppermint stick.

CHRISTMAS TREES

The Christmas season lends itself to many ideas for programs that will bring smiles and good memories to seniors. "Christmas Trees Past and Present," a program about the folklore and history of the Christmas tree, will inspire a great discussion. Bring special Christmas ornaments for the residents to see and touch and the audience will soon be talking about their family traditions and the different ways they decorated their trees. Share interesting Christmas tree trivia from the Web sites listed

---

Figure 11-2 Cinnamon ornaments are a fun volunteer project to create and make wonderfully fragrant gifts.

Cinnamon Dough Ornaments

1/2 cup cinnamon
1/2 cup store bought applesauce

Stir together with a spoon until the dough becomes stiff; use your hands to create a ball of dough.

Place the ball of dough on a sheet of waxed paper; flatten slightly with your fingers.

Place a second sheet of waxed paper over the top of the dough; roll out dough to 1/8 inch thick.

Cut shapes with cookie cutters or knife.

Poke holes in the top with a drinking straw for a hanging ribbon.

Air dry ornaments on a waxed paper covered cookie sheet for at least 24 hours until hard.

Recipe can be increased; use equal parts cinnamon and applesauce.

in the resources, make Christmas bookmarks and a Christmas word search at www.puzzlemaker.com, and provide *Eight Gifts That Don't Cost,* found at www.searchingwithin.com/reflections/gifts.html, as a handout. Everyone can sing along to favorite Christmas carols.

Make cinnamon dough ornaments ahead of time to give to each resident. Cut into Christmas shapes and tied with a red ribbon, these fragrant ornaments can be hung anywhere to decorate and scent a room. Slip one into a small plastic bag and attach the recipe on a small card for each resident.

CHRISTMAS ANIMALS

Share readings about Christmas customs and legends associated with animals for a "Christmas Animals" program. See the resource list for poems told from the point of view of the animals at the first Christmas in *Christmas in the Stable* and books about animals in Christmas songs and stories. *The Christmas Kitten* by James Herriot lends well to a discussion about receiving a pet for Christmas. Read the parts of *Twas the Night Before Christmas* that focus on Santa and the reindeer. Tell the story of how the song "Rudolph the Red-Nosed Reindeer" came to be written: the Chicago-based Montgomery Ward company had been buying and giving away coloring books for Christmas every year as a promotional gimmick, but they wanted to create their own booklet to save money. In 1939, they asked thirty-four-year-old Robert L. May to come up with a Christmas story for their coloring book *The Chain*. The audience will be interested to learn that the story and song are loosely based on *The Ugly Duckling* and that Rudolph's original name was Rollo, then Reginald. It was May's daughter who came up with the name Rudolph!

HOLIDAY JOURNEYS

"Holiday Journeys" is a discussion program about traditional winter holiday stories that involve traveling. Share favorite holiday stories and ask the audience about the most unusual place they have spent the holidays and the adventures they had getting home in time for celebrations.

CHRISTMAS FRAGRANCES

"The Fragrance of Christmas" is a program about all the good smells of the Christmas season. Bring sprigs of rosemary and pine and essential oils of frankincense and myrrh, discuss favorite holiday fragrances, share stories and props, and bring a baked treat to satisfy the senses. The resource list includes several readings for this program.

SANTA CLAUS

"Santa Claus" is a favorite topic with young and old alike. Begin the discussion with a history, favorite poems, and short stories of Santa from the resource list. Ask your audience to share some of their childhood experiences with Santa and borrow a Santa collection to show and pass around. Create a Santa word search puzzle or a Santa maze at www.puzzlemaker.com for handouts.

CHRISTMAS FAVORITES

Ask your audience to share their favorite Christmas stories, poems and carols for an easy but enjoyable "Christmas Favorites" program. Read a few children's Christmas picture books aloud. Some favorites are: *Polar Express* by Chris Van Allsburg; *Christmas Guest* by David LaRochelle; and *Jest' Fore Christmas* by Eugene Field. A humorous reading to end the program is *The Twelve Thank-You Notes of Christmas,* a reading that gives the Twelve Days of Christmas song a different twist.

Play "Name That Christmas Carol," giving the first few notes on a keyboard or piano and a clue to guess the name of the carol. After someone guesses the title, everyone can sing the carol together. If the audience seems willing, divide them into two teams to compete. A clue is given for the carol and the contestants claim how many notes they need to "Name That Christmas Carol." The team claiming the fewest

Figure 11-3 Assisted living residents enjoy a Christmas program in the community room of the facility.

Figure 11-4 Christmas Crackers can be made by volunteers and are a nice inexpensive treat.

How to Make Christmas Crackers

Cut empty paper towel rolls into 3" sections.

Cut tissue paper into 8" squares.

Wrap a paper around a roll and tie one end with an 8" piece of curling ribbon.

Place Hershey's kisses or other holiday candies into the roll.

Tie the other end with another 8" piece of curling ribbon.

Curl ribbon ends with scissors.

---

notes listens to the notes and guesses. If their guess is correct, lead them in a sing-along and then go on to the next carol. If it is incorrect, the other team gets to guess.

HOLIDAYS AROUND THE WORLD

Share the traditions and customs of other countries in "Holidays Around the World." Introduce each country by showing the traditional holiday symbols, showing and pronouncing the holiday greetings printed in large font on cards, and sharing what the seasonal weather is like during the holiday season. *Christmas Around the World* by Mary D. Lankford works well as a guide to show how several countries celebrate Christmas. Ask volunteers to help you make the holiday symbols; instructions for making them can be found in children's craft books and magazines. A globe and maps of each country are informative visual aids, too.

Christmas crackers, a European tradition, are easy, and inexpensive gifts to make for the residents. Serve wassail (from England) and stollen (from Germany) and play holiday music as refreshments are served.

For the Jewish winter holiday Hanukkah, or the Festival of Lights, tell the story of the Macabees, share the tradition of lighting the candles of the Menorah, and show how to play the Dreidel game. Serve traditional Hanukkah treats like latkes and jelly doughnuts, and give out Chocolate coins as favors.

Kwanzaa, a spiritual harvest festival with special significance to African American families, is celebrated from December 26 through January 1. Talk about the Kwanzaa tradition and make a display of the seven major symbols and explain their significance.

VIRTUAL TRAVEL

January is the perfect time for a virtual trip to an exotic place. Try a Hawaiian Luau! Give everyone a lei and a homemade flight ticket at the beginning of the program. Play Hawaiian music, give seated hula dance lessons, explain the meaning of the hand signs, and give some background history about the hula. Wear a Hawaiian print shirt and ask the nursing home staff to wear them, too. Look through the library's display decorations and ask a travel agency for tropical decorations and travel posters. A Sunshine Hanging Picture Frame, a craft project from Oriental Traders, is an inexpensive activity and souvenir. Read Hawaiian poems and the weather report for Hawaii that day, and ask residents who have been to Hawaii to share their stories with everyone. Serve pineapple chunks for a treat. Bring adult and children's books about Hawaii with lots of pictures for browsing.

John Gardner, who spoke at our library about his trip to Tristan da Cunha, inspired a virtual travel program idea for our nursing homes. Tristan da Cunha is a remote volcanic island in the South Atlantic and is the most isolated settlement in the world. Research about the island revealed a fascinating story of Corporal William Glass who settled there with his wife, two children, and two companions in the early 1800s. The island presently has about 300 inhabitants.

Show the location of your virtual destination on a map or globe, show pictures from books, postcards, and photos downloaded from the Internet, read excerpts from travelogues, and share any souvenirs you may be able to find. Serve a native snack, wear native clothing, and create a handout with facts about the people and sites. Do a whole series of travel programs for a virtual trip around the world!

TEDDY BEARS

Teddy Bears make everyone feel warm and fuzzy. Borrow Teddy bears from the children's room, family, and coworkers. Begin with a brief history of the teddy bear and ask the residents if they had—or still have—a special teddy bear. Introduce and discuss famous bears such as Paddington Bear, Winnie the Pooh, and Smokey the Bear. As you talk about each bear, offer it to someone to hold.

A Care Bear Kit can be modeled after the example in *Our Teddies, Ourselves: A Guide to the Well Bear* by Margaret and Douglas Palau. Borrow or purchase the articles needed for the kit: a children's medical kit bag, cotton stuffing, Band-Aids, an ice pack, an Ace bandage, a furmometer (a thermometer made from a popsicle stick), buttons, honey, a handkerchief, a clothespin, felt, and a paper towel roll. Hand out a small bag of Teddy Grahams for a snack and bookmarks that say "Have a Beary Nice Day!"

GROUNDHOG'S DAY

"Groundhog's Day" is a good topic for February. Information, trivia, and history can be found on the Internet at www.groundhog.org. Check out www.puzzlemaker.com for related word search puzzles and mazes to use as handouts, and look through children's books about groundhogs as a source for information and pictures for this program. Talk about Punxsutawney Phil from Punxsutawney, Pennsylvania, the world-famous weather forecasting groundhog.

VALENTINE PARTY

Warm up February with a "Be My Valentine" party at area residences. Make an easy craft project like the Valentine Wreath Kit from Oriental Traders as a Valentine keepsake and give out boxes of Sweetheart candies, stick pins that smell like roses, Valentine poems, and a Valentine word search puzzle. A sing-along to Dean Martin's "That's Amore" will make every resident feel like a Valentine.

VALENTINE HISTORY

Residents will be anxious to share some of their favorite Valentine memories. Begin a Valentine's Day program with a history of Valentine's Day, including interesting tidbits about the legends of St. Valentine, the magic spells and charms used by women to predict their future husbands, the origin of paper valentines, the American settlers and Valentine's Day, and how the verses on cards have evolved. Additional topics to discuss are the language of flowers, the Valentine symbols and their meaning, and the cost of sending a valentine then and now. Valentine trivia such as how many valentine cards are delivered annually (1,000,000,000!) add interest to the discussion.

Choose couples your residents will find familiar—movie stars and presidents and first ladies—and create a reusable poster game called "It's a Love Match." Decorate the poster with hearts, lace, and confetti, use cut out letters to write "It's a Love Match" across the top of the poster, and laminate it. Photos can be attached with tape rolls, men on one side and women on the other. Start the game with the couples mixed up and move the couples together as the residents match them. Laminating the poster makes it durable for use in several programs and from year to year—just change the pictures.

For a visual aid, make a sample love knot and a rebus Valentine message. This type of message dates back to 1641. Other visual aids can include cutout cupids, old valentine cards, handkerchiefs, heart shaped candy boxes, lace, and white gloves—all symbols of Valentine's Day. If serving refreshments, choose heart-shaped sugar cookies, party mix, and red punch. Valentine word puzzles, bookmarks, conversation heart candies, or recipes for Sweetheart Sugar Cookies are ideas for handouts.

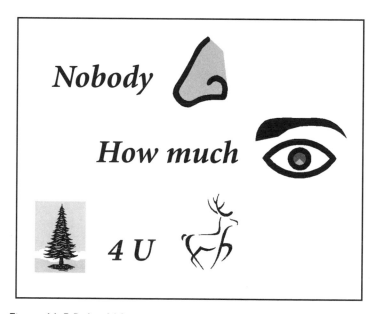

Figure 11-5 Rebus Valentines are easy to make in a word processor.

SPRING PROGRAMS

ST. PATRICK'S DAY PARTY

Green footprints leading into the community room are a cheerful invitation to a "St. Patrick's Day Party." The history of St. Patrick, Irish trivia, Irish blessings, and the legends of the shamrock, the blarney stone, and leprechauns are topics to share to begin the program. Ask the audience how many have Irish heritage or have been to Ireland. Add to the party atmosphere by serving punch and favors and by leading the group in a round of "When Irish Eyes are Smiling." Hand out a word search puzzle, crossword puzzle, and a recipe for St. Pat's Punch.

Figure 11-6 Serve this easy punch at a St. Patrick's party.

St. Patrick's Day Punch

2 64 oz. bottles white grape juice

1 12oz can frozen lemonade

1 12oz can frozen lime juice

1½ 2 liter bottles of 7up

Green food coloring, as desired, for color.

Optional: sugar, slices of lime.

NATIONAL POETRY MONTH

Celebrate April's National Poetry Month by remembering poems from the past and introducing new poetry with "Poetry Through the Ages." Everyone has grown up with poetry: Mother Goose rhymes learned as a young child, folk poetry and song rhymes learned in elementary school, required reading in high school, and favorite and popular poetry read as an adult. Some of the residents may be poets and might like to share their work. Poetry readings can be given an extra spark with a readers theatre presentation.

Make a poetry booklet handout by folding regular stock white paper in half, sandwiching the poetry pages inside a heavy stock paper cover, punching two holes along the folded side, and tying it with a ribbon. Include favorite poems and blank pages for residents to add their own poems and thoughts.

SPRING FLING

Throw a "Spring Fling" carnival with a ring toss game, a beanbag throw, and a Velcro dart game to win a small bottle of bubbles. A simple craft—Sunshine Hats from Oriental Traders—is an opportunity for the residents to be creative. Read spring poems and cheery stories, hand out a spring word search puzzle, and bring spring flower books for browsing and sharing.

WINDOW BOX GARDENING

Demonstrate ideas and tips for making window boxes for the residents' rooms with "Window Box Gardening." Make a fragrant thyme, rosemary, basil, marjoram, and sage herb garden for their community room

---

Figure 11-7 Making favors like these are good projects for teens. Make sure you provide extra kisses for them!

St. Patrick's Day Party Favors

Wrap a few Hershey's Kisses in green tulle. Print and attach this Irish verse with green ribbon:

"Just a little bit of Ireland,
That I'm sending you today,
To bring you luck and happiness,
On this fine St. Patrick's Day,
It's a wee and tiny present,
Full of luck and wishes,
Seems the little folk of Ireland,
Have sent you some Leprechaun Kisses!"

---

window using Styrofoam peanuts for drainage instead of rocks to make the box lighter, and talk about the medieval and current uses for the herbs. "I'll Plant Anything" from *Chicken Soup for the Gardeners Soul,* a story about a gardener who mistakenly plants cat poo instead of bulbs, will bring a lot of chuckles from the audience. Show books about indoor and window box gardening with pictures for browsing and checkout and make an herb word search puzzle for a handout.

THE LANGUAGE OF FLOWERS

"The Language of Flowers," a program suggestion in *Elder-Berries,* shares the history and folklore of some favorite flowers with a slide show or PowerPoint presentation of photos of the flowers. As a low-tech alternative, scan and enlarge photos of flowers to place on poster boards. Use a half sheet of poster for each flower and use both sides to make them easier to carry to the programs. Contact local florists and garden clubs to ask for fresh flower donations for the program, and they may also have someone who will speak at your programs. Bring flower and gardening books for browsing and checkout.

For a colorful matching game, laminate scanned and enlarged photos from seed catalogs or gardening books and mount them on posterboard. Print the names of the flowers and plants in large font, cut them apart, and laminate. The audience matches the names with the pictures and the presenter adheres the name to the picture with tape rolls.

CINCO DE MAYO

Fiestas, parades, mariachi music, and piñatas are ideal for Cinco de Mayo, an important Mexican-American holiday celebrating the Mexican victory over the French army on May 5, 1862. Share the history of the event, bring a piñata, wear colorful Mexican clothing, and make maracas by pouring one cup of rice into water bottles and decorating with colored paper and stickers. Play mariachi music and shake your maracas!

SUMMER PROGRAMS

STRAWBERRY FESTIVAL

CURLY Locks! Curly Locks! wilt thou be mine?
Thou shalt not wash the dishes, nor yet feed the swine,
But sit on a cushion and sew a fine seam,
And feast upon strawberries, sugar and cream....

—Mother Goose Rhyme

June is strawberry time in Ohio and the perfect time for a Strawberry Festival. Present history, trivia, medicinal uses, mythology and health and beauty tips associated with strawberries. Stimulate the senses with strawberry scented/flavored lotions, soaps, tea, Jell-O, jam, and candy. If the program is presented at an assisted living or senior apartment complex, serve strawberry shortcake, snack mix, and strawberry lemonade. Display strawberry recipe books and make recipe pamphlets

---

Figure 11-8 A refreshing treat for a strawberry festival event.

Strawberry Lemonade

Freshly squeezed juice of 9 lemons — (1½ cups)

5 – 6 cups of water

10 oz. Pkg. Frozen strawberries, pureed (fresh is fine too.)

Sugar to taste

Combine lemon juice, water and ½ of the strawberry puree. Add sugar until you have reached the desired tartness/sweetness. Add strawberry puree until the strawberry/lemon taste balance is equal.

for handouts. Fill a jar with strawberry flavored candy for a door prize or make it into a game by asking them to guess the number of candies in the jar. Adapt this same program to your area's fruit seasons.

SUMMERTIME FUN

"Summer afternoon; To me those have always been the two most beautiful words in the English language."

—Henry James

Figure 11-9 Share poems that fit the program theme.

Daffodils

I wander'd lonely as a cloud
That floats on high o'er vales and hills,
When all at once I saw a crowd,
A host, of golden daffodils;
Beside the lake, beneath the trees,
Fluttering and dancing in the breeze.

Continuous as the stars that shine
And twinkle on the Milky Way,
They stretch'd in never-ending line
Along the margin of a bay:
Ten thousand saw I at a glance,
Tossing their heads in sprightly dance.

The waves beside them danced; but they
Out-did the sparkling waves in glee:
A poet could not but be gay,
In such a jocund company:
I gazed -- and gazed -- but little thought
What wealth the show to me had brought:

For oft, when on my couch I lie
In vacant or in pensive mood,
They flash upon that inward eye
Which is the bliss of solitude;
And then my heart with pleasure fills,
And dances with the daffodils.

William Wordsworth (1770-1850)

Seniors will enjoy lively discussion as they compare the games they played as youngsters with the way young people spend their summers today in a "Summertime Fun" program. Mention timeless activities such as catching fireflies, climbing trees, and playing hopscotch, jacks, jump rope, hula hoop, pickup sticks, marbles and checkers. Bring the toys to pass around. After listening to the stories listed in the resources, everyone will enjoy singing "In the Good Old Summertime" and "Bicycle Built for Two." Hand out bookmarks, booklets of summertime songs or poems, word search puzzles, and recipes for summer treats.

A GARDEN PARTY

Residents can share pictures of gardens they have grown at "A Garden Party." During the one hour program, invite residents to wear garden hats, make a floral arrangement craft with a four-inch clay pot, floral foam, and inexpensive silk flowers, and give them tips on flower arranging. Read aloud the poem "Daffodils" by William Wordsworth, gardening jokes, and the "Top 10 Signs You Have Gone Over the Garden's Edge" from the Web sites listed in the resources. Serve sandwich cookies and punch, bring indoor gardening books and flower books for browsing, and hand out a garden word search puzzle.

FLAGS

A "Flags" program celebrates Independence Day and patriotism. Older adults are very much tuned into patriotism and are very responsive to patriotic programs. Make a poster or PowerPoint presentation of pictures of the changes in the American flag through history. Include the famous flags, "The Liberty Tree" and "Don't Tread on Me." Share the history of the flags with the residents. Cut a five point paper star with one snip of the scissors to demonstrate how Betsy Ross had convinced George Washington that the star should have five points instead of six. Talk about flag trivia and etiquette and distribute small flags to each patron.

HOT DOGS

July is National Hot Dog Month and it's amazing how much interesting trivia can be found about hot dogs! How long was the World's Longest Hot Dog? (Answer: 1,996 feet.) Did you know there is proper etiquette for eating hot dogs? DO eat hot dogs on buns with your hands. Utensils should not touch hot dogs on buns! DON'T use a cloth napkin to wipe

Figure 11-10 Scanned and enlarged flag pictures on a poster make an easy, inexpensive, and informative visual aid for the Flags program.

your mouth when eating a hot dog; paper is always preferable. Check the resources for more interesting facts to share or to create a trivia quiz.

SCHOOL DAZE

August is the perfect time to initiate discussion among nursing home residents about their school days memories with a "School Daze" program. Begin with a poem or two: *Old School Days* by Herbert J. Dance;

> **Figure 11-11 The elderly often remember and enjoy songs from their youth.**
>
> School Days
>
> School days, school days,
> Dear old Golden Rule days;
> Readin' and writin' and 'rithmatic
> Taught to the tune of a hick'ry stick
> You were my queen and calico,
> I was your bashful, barefoot beau,
> And you wrote on my slate,
> "I love you, Joe,"
> When we were a couple of kids.

The Tin Dipper by Margaret Neel; or *A Mortifying Mistake* by Anna M. Pratt. Compare one room schoolhouses to contemporary schools, give a sample lesson from the *McGuffey Reader,* and sing the "School Days" song (most of the residents will remember the words). Props and visual aids from the BiFolkal Kit or borrowed from home or coworkers can include a dinner bucket, an apple, a quill pen and ink bottle, marbles, jacks and ball, slate and chalk, a graduation cap, and pictures of one room schoolhouses. Bring McGuffey Readers for browsing and hand out bookmarks and pencils.

FALL PROGRAMS

CELEBRATE FALL

Thy bounty shines in autumn unconfined,
And speaks a common feast for all that lives.

—James Thomson

Celebrate fall with a program about all the favorite things we enjoy during the fall season. Begin by reading the poem "Then Autumn" by Garnett Ann Schultz, sharing fall pictures. Talk about apples and the many yummy ways to eat them, and follow with *An Apple a Day* by Jennifer Storey Gillis. *Johnny Appleseed* by Reeve Lindbergh tells the story of Johnny Appleseed's life in rhyme. Share the poem with another reader, alternating the verses.

Popcorn is another fall favorite, so share popcorn trivia from the Internet sites listed in the resources. A program on fall favorites wouldn't be complete without pumpkins. Favorite recipes for pumpkin pie, pumpkin trivia, and jack-o-lanterns make great topics for discussion and quizzes, and you can pass around small baskets of beautifully colored fall leaves, acorns, buckeyes, pinecones, and chestnuts and ask residents to identify them. They will enjoy the colors and textures.

Trivia games with multiple choice answers are great for encouraging the residents to participate in a discussion. They enjoy guessing the answers and feel confident when they are correct. Handouts or favors can include bookmarks, a word search puzzle, and recipes. If refreshments are served, you can't go wrong with cider, doughnuts, popcorn and candy corn. Provide fall decorations such as small gourds or pumpkins as door prizes. For Halloween, *We Celebrate Halloween: A Bobbie Kalman Book* is a good source for history and facts. Handouts can include Halloween bookmarks and word search puzzles.

TEEN READ WEEK

Celebrate Teen Read Week in October with a "Teens in the 1930s" program. During the program, compare the teens of the '30s with the teens of today. Discuss the stock market crash of 1929, the "Hoover Blanket" and "Hoovervilles"; Roosevelt and the New Deal; and the dust storms and the book and movie *The Grapes of Wrath*. Talk about the gangsters and heroes of the day and the blurred distinction between them: John Dillinger and the "woman in red," Baby Face Nelson, Bonnie and Clyde, Jesse Owens, and Amelia Earhart.

There are many interesting facts to share about food and games of the '30s. For example, the canned meat Spam first appeared during this time and the game Monopoly® was invented in 1933 by a laid-off salesman named Charles Darrow. Popular comics were Harold Teen, Blondie and Dagwood, Little Orphan Annie, Dick Tracy, and Terry and the Pirates. Radio was the most popular media, and favorite programs included Amos and Andy, Jack Benny, Fibber McGee and Molly, Edgar Bergen and Charlie McCarthy.

Write slang words on poster cards so that the residents can see them and ask if they remember using them. Some examples are: "a scream," "a hoot," "jack," "cheese it," "yowsah," "the eagers," "the big it," and "fogbound." Ask teens in the library what slang words are being used today for comparison. Be sure to show the books and movies that were popular in the '30s in case anyone would like check them out. Use comic books, a can of spam, and audiotapes of radio shows as visual and audio aids and make a 1930s word search puzzle to hand out at the end of the program.

NATIONAL CHILDREN'S BOOK WEEK

National Children's Book Week in November provides an excellent time to round up your favorite children's books, take them to the facilities to share with the residents, and keep them up to date with what children are reading today. Check the lists in Appendix E for many children's books that seniors will enjoy. Short, humorous, heartwarming, or just plain silly stories with wonderful illustrations are enjoyable for any age. Include a brief explanation of why we celebrate National Children's Book Week, talk about the children's department and the programs that are taking place, and include statistics regarding how many children's books have been checked out during the month and

Figure 11-12 The Peterborough Town Library organized a reading club at a local residential facility. The readers enjoy reading the children's literature they hear about on TV and NPR.

year-to-date and how many children have attended the story times. Give each person in the audience a children's bookmark.

THANKSGIVING

Thanksgiving programs can be a mixture of tradition and fun. Begin with the story of Squanto, the Indian that saved the pilgrims from starvation. Use turkey trivia for a discussion or quiz: How many feathers do turkeys have at maturity? (Answer: 3,499.) How fast can a turkey trot? (Answer: 25 mph.) Introduce the little-known Thanksgiving tradition from the late 1850s of placing of five kernels of corn beside each plate and naming a blessing for each one. *The Iroquois Prayer*, *Over the River and Through the Woods* and *Twas the Night Before Thanksgiving* are excellent read-aloud stories for this program and a "Turkey Time" crossword puzzle, bookmarks, or Thanksgiving lapel pins make nice handouts.

READ-ALOUD PROGRAMS

Read-aloud programs have been successful for nursing homes, Alzheimer patients, adult day care, personal care homes, and assisted living facilities. They can be presented by a member of the library staff or, for a special treat, a local celebrity or a visiting author. Read the material before the program to know how much time to allow for reading and discussion. A half-hour of sustained reading is plenty, and if a longer program is needed, add other activities.

Adapt the read-aloud programs to your audience. For example, a book that continues from week to week may inspire speculation and discussion among the younger seniors, while some elderly residents would enjoy short stories and poems that can be finished in one sitting and may not be able to remember a story from one visit to the next. Some audiences will enjoy a "round robin" read-aloud, where every participant reads a portion of the story. Read slowly and clearly, changing your tone and expression to make your voice fit the material, and ask your audience to raise a hand if you are reading too softly or quickly. If you are reading a continuing story, spend the first few minutes talking about the previous reading and ask for thoughts from the audience about what is going to happen. Bring props for the readings and pass out bookmarks or other handout as a souvenir of the program. See Appendix E for lists of favorite read-aloud books suggested by our contributors.

MORE BOOK AND READING PROGRAM IDEAS

- Hold monthly "Share-a-Read" groups at senior residential facilities. The participants talk about their reading experiences on a given genre, author, or subject theme and can decide together what the next month's assignment will be.

- Start a Summer Library Club and give a small award and a certificate to all residents who attend all of the summer library programs presented at their residence.

- Visit senior centers each month to book-talk, sign up patrons for library cards, lead book discussions, and bring special requests.

- Focus on the life and work of one author with visual aids to outline a biography. An example is Laura Ingalls Wilder; wear or display a period costume while talking about her life and writing, using a *McGuffey's Reader*, a slate with chalk, a tin lunch pail with an apple, a pair of spectacles, and the books by Laura Ingalls Wilder as props. Are there famous authors from your area that would make interesting topics for a program?

- Start a reading group with a focus on children's literature so seniors can read the books they enjoyed or missed as children. They may want to read what their grandchildren are reading or books they hear about on television and radio. Harry Potter and Lemony Snicket books are fun to read at any age.

- Take your library's summer reading program to the senior residences. Each book, audio or video the patrons check out counts as an entry for the end of the summer drawing for prizes.

- Begin a reading incentive program for summer or anytime. Provide reading logs for your senior patrons and award small incentive prizes for every five books read. Grand prizes can be awarded in a final drawing at the end of the program.

- Sponsor a professional storytelling troupe to visit area nursing homes and senior facilities, adapting

Figure 11-13 Arthur was a welcome guest at our local nursing homes.

their programs to the audience and presenting animated stories embellished with props. Invite one of the children's story time groups to meet at a nursing home for a fun intergenerational program that will make your programming dollars go farther.

- Rent book character costumes for someone to wear for a story time. Libraries often do this for children, but the nursing home residents in our area really enjoyed a visit from "Arthur," a character from the books by Marc Brown. The costumes can be hot and claustrophobic for the wearer, so keep visits short, but busy. The character should not talk, but be animated. The program can begin with a story and background about the main character; then the surprise costumed guest can arrive, shake hands, and interact with the audience. He can act out part of a story as it is read aloud, dance, or do whatever suits the character's personality. After he waves good-bye with enthusiasm, ask the residents who their favorite book characters were when they were young.

- Invite local craftspeople to share their handicrafts with your seniors. Carry the handicrafts around to each resident so they may look closely, touch, and appreciate the work. Quilters, needleworkers, woodcarvers, beadworkers and many other crafters enjoy sharing their work and talking about their craft, and your coworkers, friends and family may also be sources for a variety of crafts and hobbies to show and share. Easy craft projects that can be completed in a visit add hands-on experience and make a remembrance for the program.

NAME THAT BIRD

Play a "Name That Bird" game using bird books with companion recordings of bird songs. Play the bird songs one at a time, show a picture of the bird, and ask the audience to guess the name of the bird. Bring ingredients for one of the recipes from the Web site listed in the resources and make a treat for the birds for a hands-on project. Ask staff to hang the bird treats outside the residents' windows.

JEOPARDY

Make a reusable, portable Jeopardy game board with a folding science fair display board. Start by gluing colored cut-out letters spelling "Jeopardy" across the center top edge of the board. With a straightedge and permanent marker, draw a line across the board under the title and draw lines to divide the board into four columns. Draw another line across the board about three inches below the first to label the categories. Divide the rest of the board into five rows to create the boxes for the questions. Cover the entire board with clear Contact paper. Post-it paper or paper with masking tape rolls can now be attached, moved, and removed easily.

Decide on a main subject, think of four categories about that subject, and choose four colors of pastel paper, one for each category. Write or type the categories on paper cut to fit the category heading boxes and tape them to the top of each column. Compose twenty questions, five for each category, and label them by point value: 100, 200, 300, 400, and 500. Type or write the answers for each question in large font on the bottom half of a sheet of paper, labeling each answer A, B, C, and D. Fold the top of the paper over the answers and write the point value on the front and tape to the board in the appropriate box. The top corners of the board can be decorated with words or pictures to show the subject of the game.

Multiple-choice questions are easier than the traditional Jeopardy format, and adding a few humorous wrong answers will prompt some laughter. Divide the audience into two teams and select two people to be

Figure 11-14 A laminated Jeopardy game board can be adapted to any trivia topic.			
Jeopardy			
Category 1	Category 2	Category 3	Category 4

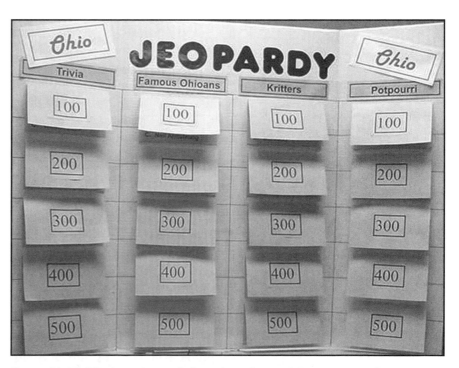

Figure 11-15 The basic Jeopardy board can be used for any trivia theme.

the team leaders. The team leader picks the category and number of points, the programmer reads the question and reveals the possible answers, and the team works together to answer the question. A timer is optional. If they miss the question, the other team gets a chance to answer. You can use this game for any occasion, using trivia and facts on any topic. "Global Jeopardy" fit in with an international summer reading theme, "Famous Women" worked well for National Women's Month, and Ohio Jeopardy is part of the Ohio Bicentennial programming for nursing homes. Provide inexpensive prizes for the winning team.

FAMOUS AMERICAN ARTISTS

"Grandma Moses" is a topic for a thirty-minute program described in *Elder-Berries*. Pass around prints of her paintings, read selections from her biography, and discuss the accomplishments of other older adults. Norman Rockwell and Frederic Remington are two more suggestions for American artist programs. Tell about their inspirations to begin painting, interesting events in their lives, and facts about their home towns.

SPACE

Build a program around the library's summer reading theme. For a space-themed program for "Reading is Out of this World," show pictures and posters of the solar system, planets, and stars; talk about the history of space travel, famous astronauts, and current space missions; and share space trivia such as the average time it takes different planets to revolve around the sun and the average temperature of different planets. Figuring your age and weight on other planets compared to Earth is a fun activity. For handouts, create a word search puzzle and a space maze at www.puzzlemaker.com.

CIRCUS

A library developed a Circus program to coincide with the summer reading theme, "Your Library: The Greatest Show in Town." For a similar program, begin by asking residents if they have ever been to a circus or remember the circus coming to town. After discussing their experiences, continue with a brief history of the circus. Include interesting facts about the three types of clowns—whiteface, auguste, and character—talk about their different roles in the circus, and the costumes and dressing rooms that they use. The folklore of Pink Lemonade is another fun and little-known tale. It is fun to use for games and discussion. Print words from circus lingo, the language of the circus people, on poster board flash cards to show the residents how the words are spelled as you explain their pronunciation and meaning, or make a matching game to let the audience guess what the words mean. Circus resources are listed at the end of this chapter.

Borrow summer reading ideas from other departments in the library. "Intermission," a matching game of circus food pictures with food trivia printed on balloon shapes, was borrowed from the young adult department. For the game "Under the Big Top," print circus superstition questions on tent shapes, glue the top edges of the tents to a poster, and list the multiple-choice answers to the questions under the tents. Read the questions, lift the tent to read the choices, and let residents guess which answer is correct. Offer circus word puzzles or mazes, clown bookmarks, and circus peanuts in snack bags as handouts.

SPICES AND HERBS

Residents will enjoy a "Spices and Herbs" program. Put twelve different spices and herbs in separate zip lock bags and number them. Make a master list of the numbers and spices for yourself. Pass the spices around the audience and ask them to guess what each one is, first by sight and then by smell. As each spice returns to you, identify it, show a picture of the plant, tell where it grows and the traditional uses. Create a SPICE Bingo game with the names of spices and herbs, using Bingomaker software. Award individual orange spice tea bags for prizes.

CHOCOLATE

Life is like a box of chocolates—you never know what you're going to get.

—Forrest Gump in *Forrest Gump*

Not only is a Chocolate program fun, but it smells and tastes good, too. The presentation can include chocolate quotes like the one from *Forrest Gump*, chocolate trivia (Americans eat about ten pounds of chocolate a year per capita, the Swiss eat twenty-two pounds), and the rules for eating chocolate (If you've got melted chocolate all over your hands, you're eating it too slowly!). A chocolate quiz invites audience participation. Can you guess how many chocolate bars the largest chocolate factory makes each year: (a) over a million, (b) over a billion, or (c) over a trillion? (The answer, in case you're wondering, is B.) The perfect handout is chocolate, of course. If the setting allows for a party, make chocolate fondue by melting a bag of semi-sweet chocolate chips and stirring in one half cup of whipping cream. If you don't

Figure 11-16 Create a Spice It Up Bingo Card for the Spice Program. Bingo cards can be created around many themes using Bingomaker software.

S	P	I	C	E
Parsley	Thyme	Oregano	Pepper	Bay Leaves
Celery Seed	Cinnamon	Fennel	Nutmeg	Paprika
Rosemary	Garlic	Free Space	Cloves	Mustard Seed
Sage	Tarragon	Curry	Tumeric	Allspice
Basil	Cayenne	Caraway Seed	Ginger	Cilantro

have a fondue pot, keep it warm in a small crock pot or over hot water in a chafing dish. Dip cubes of pound cake, fruit chunks, and pretzels. Check the resources for Web sites and books to satisfy the chocoholics in your audience.

BASEBALL

Even if you're not a fan, "Baseball" can be a fun program in the summertime or before the World Series. Share a bit of history and fun facts about baseball. Just about everyone has an opinion about a favorite player or team or a fond memory of playing the game themselves; ask to hear personal experiences, talk about the home teams in your area, and talk about baseball legends like Babe Ruth. Wear a baseball hat and/or shirt, borrow baseball items from baseball fans, and show pictures of famous players as visual aids. Don't forget to sing "Take Me Out to the Ball Game!" Cracker Jacks are a great handout.

Figure 11-17 Creative poems can be found on the Internet to use in programs.

A Chocolate Poem

By the shores of Gitchee Gumee,
By the shining chocolate water,
Stood the truffles and the brownies,
Chocolate chips inside the brownies,
Dark behind them rose the layer cake,
Rose the dark and chocolate flour dough,
Rose the creamy mocha frosting;
Bright before it flowed the chocolate,
Flowed the rich and sensuous chocolate,
Flowed the shining chocolate water…..

By Henry Wadsworth Longfellow
and Peter Mansbach

www.pmansbach.com/choc.html

GUEST SPEAKERS

The Columbus Zoo has a "Senior Safari" outreach program that visits nursing homes, assisted living, retirement homes, and senior centers within sixty-five miles of the zoo. Seven small to medium sized animals are brought to the facility for a hands-on experience. Contact the nearest zoo or nature center to ask about similar programs, and offer to coordinate a visit with the senior facilities in your area.

The Loudon County Public Library has created two significant series of programs through grants. "Fast Forward—Science Technology and the Communication Revolution," funded by the National Science Foundation, the Alfred P. Sloan Foundation, and the National Endowment for the Humanities, was a six-part series using documentary films and text to explore the impact of science and technology in the twentieth century, including radio, television, telephone, movies, and the Internet. Loudon County Public Library was one of only twelve libraries nationwide selected to receive funding from the Robert Woods Johnson Foundation for "On Our Own Terms: Moyers on Dying in America," a six-part series about dying and care at the end of life as dealt with by individuals and the country.. Reading, discussion, panel

> **Figure 11-18 Another song seniors will know from their youth.**
>
> Take Me Out to the Ballgame
> Take me out to the ball-game,
> Take me out to the park
> Buy me some peanuts and cracker jack
> I don't care if I never come back,
> Let me root root root for the home team,
> If they don't win it's a shame.
> For it's one, two, three strikes,
> "You're out!" at the old ball – game.

programs, a National Issues Forum, participation by local authorities, and community action development were included in the program. Rabbi Harold S. Kushner, author of *When Bad Things Happen to Good People,* was the featured speaker.

RESIDENTS IN THE LIBRARY

Nursing homes are required to provide outings for residents who are able to go out into the community. The library is a perfect stop for them, and scheduling a program just for their visit will make it memorable and special.

Invite the residents to a "Senior Tea" each spring. The size of the meeting room will determine how many guests you can invite at one time; require reservations so the room can be set up to accommodate wheelchairs and to allow room for assistants, and offer the program more than once if you have a large potential guest list, or rotate the invitation among the facilities each year. A speaker can present a short program on a variety of topics such as growing and using herbs, making soap, and collecting dolls. Decorate tables with teapots and pretty flowery and lacey paper goods to make the room look special, and serve a variety of teas with dainty sandwiches, pretty cookies and fresh fruit. More information on tea party program themes is available in Chapter 4.

A summer "Picnic on the Deck" (or patio or lawn) of your library is a pleasant outdoor activity for visiting nursing home residents. Ask the facilities to provide sack or box lunches for their residents, and the library can provide beverages, stories, and readers theatre plays.

Figure 11-19 Nursing home residents enjoy an outing at the library for a Picnic on the Deck.

Library staff, volunteers, or teen groups can help present the story as a readers theatre. Books and Web sites in the resources offer stories already scripted, but you can adapt other stories once you have experience.

Holiday decorations and refreshments make the library's holiday parties described earlier in this chapter ideal for nursing home residents. Any library presentations that include speakers and authors should try to accommodate seniors and nursing home residents; send an invitation to the facilities in your community to inform them of a wonderful opportunity for their residents and to let them know the program setting will accommodate their needs. Be sure the event is handicapped accessible and that adequate space is available to accommodate wheelchairs and assistants.

RESOURCES

FOR OVERVIEW:

1. Trotta, Marcia. 1993. *Managing Library Outreach Programs: a How-To-Do-It Manual for Librarians.* New York: Neal-Schuman.

2. Dye, Lee. "Music and the Brain Are Brains Wired for Music Better Built to Last?" ABCNEWS.com http://abcnews.go.com/sections /scitech/DyeHard/dyehard020123.html.

FOR REMEMBERING:

1. Buchanan, Diane, RN, DNSc, Lucy Cabico, RN, MScN, and Donna Spevakow, RN, MSN. "Reminiscing: An Approach to Help Older Adults Stay Connected." Stride. www.stridemagazine.com/ 2001_Aug/ buchanan/buchanan.htm.

FOR HANDY KITCHEN GADGETS:

1. Celchar, Jane H. 1982. *Kitchen and Gadgets—1920–1950.* Radnor, PA: Wallace-Homestead Book.
2. Kalman, Bobbie. 1990. *The Kitchen.* Toronto: Crabtree.
3. Lindenberger, Jan. 1996. *Fun Kitchen Collectibles.* Atglen, PA: Schiffer.
4. Huntington, Sharon. "How Table Manners Became Polite." The Christian Publishing Society. http://csmweb2.emcweb.com/durable/ 2000/11/28/fp22s1-csm.shtml.
5. Kitchen Trivia circa 1500s. http://members.aol.com/AltMartha/ Trivia1500s.index.html.

FOR APRONS:

1. Brillhart, Julie.1990. *Anna's Goodbye Apron.* Niles, IL: A. Whitman.
2. Cheney, Joyce. 2000. *Aprons — Icons of the American Home.* Philadelphia, PA: Running Press Book Publishers.
3. McKissack, Patricia C. 1997. *Ma Dear's Aprons.* New York: Atheneum Books for Young Readers.
4. "My Ode to Grandma's Apron." http://patsyrose224.tripod.com/ apron.html.
5. "Sweet Memories Are Tied In Apron Strings." *Reminisce Magazine.* (May/June 99) :32–33.

FOR WINTER:

1. Bentley, W.A., and W. J. Humphreys. 1962. *Snow Crystals.* New York: Dover Publications.
2. Cuyler, Margery. 1998. *The Biggest, Best Snowman.* New York: Scholastic.
3. Frost, Robert. 2001. *Stopping by Woods on a Snowy Evening.* New York: Dutton Children's Books.
4. Kirk, Daniel. 2000. *The Snow Family.* New York: Hyperion Books for Children.

5. Martin, Jacqueline Briggs. 1998. *Snowflake Bentley*. Boston: Houghton Mifflin.

6. "Paper Snowflakes: My Web3000.com. www.myweb3000.com/snowflakes.html.

FOR CHRISTMAS TREES

1. Bunting,Eve. 1991. *Night Tree*. San Diego: Harcourt Brace Jovanovich.

2. *Diane Goode's American Christmas*. 1990. New York: Dutton Children's Books.

3. "Christmas Trees and More." University of Illinois Extension. www.urbanext.uiuc.edu/trees/index.html.

4. Discovery School's Puzzlemaker. Discovery.com. http://puzzlemaker.school.discovery.com.

5. "Eight Gifts That Don't Cost a Cent." www.searching within.com/ reflections/gifts.html.

6. Sicard, Cheri. "The History of Christmas Trees." Enigma Communications. www.fabulousfoods.com/holidays/xmas/tree history.html.

FOR CHRISTMAS ANIMALS:

1. Barth, Edna. 2000. *Holly, Reindeer and Colored Lights: the Story of Christmas Symbols*. New York: Clarion Books.

2. Herriot, James. 1996. *The Christmas Day Kitten*. New York: St. Martin's Press.

3. Krutch, Joseph W. 1976. *Wildlife Christmas Treasury*. National Wildlife Federation.

4. Lindgren, Astrid. 1962. *Christmas in the Stable*. New York: Coward-McCann.

5. Sechrist, Elizabeth Hough. 1959. *It's Time for Christmas*. Philadelphia: Macrae Smith.

6. Webster, Barbara. 1954. *Creatures and Contentments; Ruminations on Living in the Country*. New York: Norton.

7. Yolen, Jane. 1991. *Hark, A Christmas Sampler*. New York: Putnam.

8. Brain, Marshall. "Who is this Reindeer named Rudolph?" *HowStuffWorks*. www.howstuffworks.com/christmas20.htm.

FOR FRAGRANCE OF CHRISTMAS:

1. Dickens, Charles. 1906. "Cratchit's Dinner" *A Christmas Carol*. Scott, Foresman and Co.

2. Simmons, Adelma Grenier. 1968. *A Merry Christmas Herbal.* New York: W. Morrow.

FOR SANTA:

1. Chris, Teresa. 1992. *The Story of Santa Claus.* New Jersey: Chartwell Books.
2. Church, Francis Pharcellus. 1992. *Yes, Virginia There is a Santa Claus.* New York: Delacorte Press.
3. Gibbons, Gail. 1999. *Santa Who?* New York: Morrow Junior Books.
4. LaRochelle, David. 1988. *Christmas Guest.* Minneapolis: Carolrhoda Books.
5. Moore, Clement Clarke. 1991. *The Grandma Moses Night Before Christmas.* New York: Random House.
6. Rockwell, Molly, ed. *Norman Rockwell's Christmas Book.*1977. New York: H. N. Abrams.
7. Van Allsburg, Chris. 1985. *The Polar Express.* Boston: Houghton Mifflin.
8. Field, Eugene. "Jest' Fore Christmas." Poet's Corner. www.theotherpages.org/poems/field01.html.
9. "The Twelve Thank-You Notes of Christmas." www.geoci ties.com/Heartland/Fields/8616/christmas/thankyou.html.

FOR HOLIDAY TRADITIONS:

1. "The Jewish Holiday of Hanukkah" www.hanukkah-tradi tions.com/
2. "Kwanzaa Information Center" www.melanet.com/kwanzaa/ home.html

FOR VIRTUAL TRIP:

1. Hosegood, Nancy. 1966. *Corporal Glass's Island; the Story of Tristan da Cunha.* New York: Farrar, Straus, and Giroux.
2. Munch, Peter Andreas. 1971. *Crisis in Untopia; The Ordeal of Tristan da Cunha.* New York: Crowell.
3. Whiteside, Thomas. 1964. *Alone Through the Dark Sea.* New York: Braziller.
4. Baldwin, Brian. "Tristan da Cunha, South Atlantic Ocean." (January 2003) http://website.lineone.net/~sthelena/tristaninfo.htm.
5. "Tristan da Cunha History." www.btinternet.com/~sa_sa/tris tan_da_cunha/tristan_history.html

6. Dance Instruction and Demonstration Videos. www.myriahs .com/publishvideos/instruction.html.

7. Ekwall, John and Jan Tunér. "Tristan da Cunha." www.sthele na.se/tristan/tristan.htm.

8. Hula Dance Videos. www.centralhome.com/ballroomcountry/ hula_dance_videos.htm.

9. Oriental Trading Company Inc. www.oriental.com.

10. Weaver, Barry. "Tristan da Cunha." University of Oklahoma. http://geowww.gcn.ou.edu/~bweaver/Ascension/tdc.htm.

FOR TEDDY BEARS:

1. Bond, Michael. 1998. *Paddington Bear*. HarperCollins.

2. Friedman, Sharon and Irene Shere. 1986. *Grin and Bear it! Jokes about Teddy Bears*. Minneapolis: Lerner Publications.

3. Milne, A. A. 2001. *The Complete Tales and Poems of Winnie the Pooh*. New York: Dutton Children's Books.

4. Murphy, Frank. 2000. *The Legend of the Teddy Bear*. Chelsea, Michigan: Sleeping Bear Press.

5. Palau, Margaret and Douglas. *Our Teddies, Ourselves: A Guide to the Well Bear*.

6. Theobalds, Prue, comp. 1989. *The Teddy Bear: An Anthology*. London: New York: Blackie; Bedrick/Blackie.

7. Brehm, Kelly Brown. "A General History of the Teddy Bear." BrownBrehm Bears. www.teddybears.com/history/tgth15.htm.

8. "History of Rupert Bear." www.teddy-bear-uk.com/learning/ famous/rupert/history.htm.

9. "Teddybears History 1902–2002." www.cobweb.nl/wcoumans/ tedhist.htm.

FOR GROUNDHOG'S DAY:

1. "The Official Site of the Punxsutawney Groundhog Club." Groundhog.org. www.groundhog.org.

FOR VALENTINE'S DAY:

1. Brown, Fern G. 1983. *Valentine's Day*. New York: F. Watts.

2. Kalman, Bobbie.1986. *We Celebrate Valentine's Day*. Toronto/New York: Crabtree.

3. Tabori, Lena, and Natasha Tobori Fried, eds. 2000. *The Little Big Book of Love*. New York: William Morrow.

4. "Annie's Valentine History Page." www.annieshome page.com/valhistory.html.

5. "Valentines Day History." www.pictureframes.co.uk/pages/saint_valentine.htm.

6. *Valentine's Day Actiphile*. Madison, Wisconsin: BiFolkal Productions.

FOR ST. PATRICK'S DAY:

1. Gibbons, Gail. 1994. *St. Patrick's Day*. New York: Holiday House.

2. *St. Patrick's Day Actiphile*. 2000. Madison: BiFolkal Productions.

FOR POETRY:

1. Longfellow, Henry Wadsworth. *Favorite Poems of Henry Wadsworth Longfellow*. 1947. Garden City, NY: Doubleday.

2. Felleman, Hazel. 1936. *The Best Loved Poems of the American People*. Garden City, NY: Doubleday.

3. Longworth, Alice Roosevelt, comp. 1941. *Desk Drawer Anthology*. Garden City, NY: Garden City Publisher.

4. Martz, Sandra, ed. 1991. *When I Am an Old Woman, I Shall Wear Purple*. Watsonville, CA: Papier-Mache Press.

5. Martz, Sandra Haldeman, ed. 1992. *If I Had My Live to Live Over, I would Pick More Daisies*. Watsonville, CA: Papier-Mache Press.

6. *Mother Goose: A Collection of Classic Nursery Rhymes*. 1984. New York: Henry Holt

7. Schwarz, Alvin. 1992. *And the Green Grass Grew All Around: Folk Poetry from Everyone*. New York: HarperCollins.

8. Silverstein, Shel. 1981. *A Light in the Attic*. New York: Harper and Row.

FOR SPRING FLING:

1. Oriental Trading Company Inc. www.oriental.com.

FOR CINCO DE MAYO

1. Cinco de Mayo at Web Holidays www.web-holidays.com/demayo/index.asp

FOR WINDOW BOX:

1. Wilcox, Valerie. 2000. "I'll Plant Anything.*" Chicken Soup for the Gardeners Soul*. Deerfield Beach, FL: Health Communications.

FOR STRAWBERRIES:

1. Bruchac, Joseph. 1993. *The First Strawberries—A Cherokee Story*. New York: Dial Books for Children.
2. Busenberg, Bonnie. 1994. *Vanilla, Chocolate and Strawberry: The Story of Your Favorite Flavors*. Minneapolis: Lerner Publications.
3. Coldrey, Jennifer. 1989. *Strawberry*. Englewood, NJ: Silver Burdett Press.
4. Whitaker, Stafford. 1985. *The Compleat Strawberry*. New York: Crown Publishers.
5. Strawberry JAMM. "Strawberry Harvests and Horticulture." www.jamm.com/strawberry/harvests.html.

FOR GARDEN PARTY:

1. "Martha Stewart Parody." www.geocities.com/Hollywood/Boulevard/8005/sitemapp.html.
2. The Gardeners Network. "Garden Fun and Games." www.gardenersnet.com/fun.htm.

FOR SUMMERTIME FUN:

1. Hopkins, Lee Bennett. 1990. *Good Books, Good Times*. New York: Harper and Row.
2. Read, Hadley. 1977. *Morning Chores and Other Times Remembered*. Urbana: University of Illinois Press.
3. Teale, Edwin Way. 1960. *Journey into Summer*. New York: Dodd, Mead.
4. Wallace, Mary. 1997. *Summer Magic*. Garden City, NY: Doubleday.
5. "What Shall I Pack in the Box Called Summer?" and "How Hot Was It?" *Remembering Summer*. Madison, WI: BiFolkal Productions Manual.

FOR FLAGS:

1. Armbuster, Ann. 1991. *The American Flag*. New York: Franklin Watts.

2.   Fradin, Dennis B. 1989. *The Flag of the United States*. Chicago: Children's Press.

3.   Loomis, Christine. 2000. *Across America—I Love You*. New York: Hyperion Press for Children.

4.   West, Delno C., and Jean M. West. 2000. *Uncle Sam and Old Glory: Symbols of America*. New York: Atheneum Books for Young Readers.

5.   Independence Hall Association. "Flag Trivia." www.ushistory.org/betsy/flagtriv.html.

6.   Streufert, Duane. "The Flag of the United States." www.usflag.org/toc.html.

FOR HOT DOGS:

1.   National Hot Dog and Sausage Council. "Facts and Trivia." www.hot-dog.org.

2.   Hot Dog Jonny's. "Hot Dog Etiquette." www.hotdogjonnys.com/etiquette.htm.

FOR SCHOOL DAZE:

1.   Fulghum, Robert. 1988. *All I Really Need to Know I Learned in Kindergarten*. New York: Villard Books.

2.   Grove, Myrna J. 2000. *Legacy of One-Room Schools*. Morgantown, PA: Masthof Press.

3.   Houston, Gloria. 1992. *My Great Arizona*. New York: HarperCollins Children's Books.

4.   Kalman, Bobbie. 1994. *A One Room School (Historic Communities)*. New York: Crabtree.

5.   McGuffey, William Holmes. 1879. *McGuffey's Readers*. Rev. ed. New York: American Book.

6.   Sathoff, Craig E. 1996. "School Days, Country Style." *Ideals,* September.

7.   Seuss, Dr., and Jack Prelutsky. 1998. *Hooray for Diffendoofer Day*. New York: Knopf.

8.   Windscheffel, Gerhard "Wally." 1997. "First Day at School." *Good Old Days*. (September).

9.   Dance, Herbert J. "Old School Days" *Remembering School Days*. Madison, WI: BiFolkal Productions.

10. Neel, Margaret, "The Tin Dipper" *Remembering School Days*. Madison, WI: BiFolkal Productions.

11 *School Days Actiphile*. Madison, WI: BiFolkal Productions.

FOR HALLOWEEN:

1. Kalman, Bobbie. 1985. *We Celebrate Halloween*. Toronto/New York: Crabtree.
2. Leech, Maria. 1982. *The Thing at the Foot of the Bed and Other Scary Stories*. New York: Philomel Books.
3. Wallace, Daisy, ed. 1979. *Ghost Poems*. New York: Holiday House.
4. Wallace, Daisy, ed.1976. *Witch Poems*. New York: Holiday House.
5. Riley, James Whitcomb. "Little Orphant Annie." Geometry. www.poetry-archive.com/r/little_orphant_annie.html.
6. Riley, James Whitcomb. "Old October" Poetry for Autumn. www.geocities.com/beccisgirls/autumn.html.

FOR FALL:

1. White, Linda. 1996. *Too Many Pumpkins*. New York: Holiday House.
2. Sathoff, Craig E. 1999. "In Praise of Pumpkins." *Ideals*, September.
3. The Popcorn Poppery. "Fun, Facts and Trivia." www.popcorn poppery.com/fun.html.
4. Swan Pumpkin Farm. "Making Pumpkin Time the Best Time." www.thepumpkinfarm.com.
5. The Popcorn Board. "Popcorn!" www.popcorn.org.
6. Great Plains KettleKorn "Popcorn Trivia." www.greatplains kettlekorn.com/trivia.htm.
7. Jefferson Middle School Library. "Pumpkin Trivia." http://tjms2.jefferson.arlington.k12.va.us/Class_Projects/Pumpkin_triv ia/pumpkin_trivia.html.
8. Long Island Gardening. "Pumpkin Trivia." www.ligar dening.com/Pages/Article.cfm?ID=128&CurrArticlePage=4.
9. Riley, James Whitcomb. "When the Frost is on the Pumpkin." Bartleby.com www.bartleby.com/104/10.htmland.

FOR TEENS IN THE 1930S:

1. Rollin, Lucy. 1999. *Twentieth-Century Teen Culture by the Decades, A Reference Guide*. West Port, CT: Greenwood Press.

FOR THANKSGIVING:

1. Pilkey, Dav. 1990. *Twas the Night Before Thanksgiving*. New York: Orchard Books.
2. Fuller, Letha. 1998. "Thanksgiving." *Good Old Days,* November: 7.
3. Legend of the Five Kernels. http://arose4ever.com/karen/thanksgiv/5kernels.htm.
4. Woodbridge Vintage Barrel Chips. "Turkey Trivia." www.woodbridgechips.com/turkeytrivia.html.
5. Turkey Trivia Quiz. www.care2.com/community/trivia/trivia_9911.html.
6. *Thanksgiving Actiphile*. Madison, WI: BiFolkal Productions.

FOR LAURA INGALLS WILDER:

1. Anderson, William. 1989. *Little House Country*. Kansas City, MO: Terrell.
2. Collins, Carolyn Strom, and Christina Wyss Ericksson. 1996. *The World of Little House*. New York: HarperCollins.
3. Hines, Stephen W. 1994. *I Remember Laura*. Nashville: T. Nelson.
4. Wilder, Laura Ingalls, adapted. 1995. *My Little House Songbook*. New York: HarperCollins.
5. Irby, Rebecca LeeAnne and Phil Greetham. "Laura Ingalls Wilder: Frontier Girl." http://webpages.marshall.edu/~irby1/laura.htmlx

FOR NAME THAT BIRD:

1. *The Bird Watcher's Library*. 1989. New York: Gallery Books.
2. Birding/Wild Birds. "Cooking FOR the Birds—Recipe Collection." http://birding.about.com/library/weekly/aa031300a.htm.
3. Elliott, Lang. 1991. *Know Your Bird Sounds*. Ithaca, NY: NatureSound Studio. Audio Cassette/Book.

FOR GRANDMA MOSES:

1. Moses, Grandma. 1946. *Grandma Moses, American Primitive*. New York: Dryden Press.

FOR HATS:

1. Howard, Elizabeth Fitzgerald. 1991. *Aunt Flossie's Hats (and crab cakes later)*. New York: Clarion Books.
2. Karon, Jan. 2001. *Miss Fannie's Hat*. New York: Puffin Books.
3. Seuss, Dr. 1938. *The 500 Hats of Bartholomew Cubbins*. New York: Vanguard Press.
4. Seuss, Dr. 1957. *The Cat in the Hat*. New York: Random House.
5. Slobodkina, Esphyr. 1985. *Caps for Sale*. New York: Harper and Row.
6. "Come Along and Remember: When Hats Were Tops." 1999. *Reminisce,* March/April: 8–11.
7. Yablonsky, Margie. 2000. "The Hat Syndrome." *Good Old Days,* February: 36–37.
8. Davidson, Jan. "Brief History of 20th Century Hats." Custom Millinery. www.hatshatshats.com/history.htm.

FOR OLD-TIME RADIO:

1. Buxton, Frank, and Bill Owen. 1972. *The Big Broadcast 1920–1950*. New York: Viking Press.
2. French, Jack. 1997. "Sound Effects." The Original Old Time Radio WWW Pages. www.old-time.com/sfx.html.
3. L.O.F. Communications. "The Nostalgia Pages." www.lof com.com/ nostalgia.
4. Wisconsin Electronic Reader Gallery: Radio. www.library. wisc.edu/etext/WIReader/Galleries/Radio.html.

FOR SPACE:

1. Enchanted Learning. "What Would Your Age Be On Other Planets?" www.ZoomSchool.com/subjects/astronomy/age.shtml.
2. Zoom Astronomy. www.EnchantedLearning.com/subjects/ astronomy.

FOR CIRCUS:

1. Granfield, Linda. 1998. *Circus: an Album*. New York: DK Ink.
2. Otis, James. 1947. *Toby Tyler Ten Weeks with a Circus*. Cleveland/New York: World Publishing.
3. Hanneford Family Circus. "A Brief History of the Early Circus." www.hanneford.8m.com/history/early_history.htm.
4. Intelligent Software Associates. 1996. "Circus History." www.circusweb.com/cwhistory.html.

5. Big Top Productions. 1995. "Circus Lingo." http://anduin.eldar.org/~ben/funny/html/254.html.

6. Circus Trivia. www.shrinecircusduluth.com/links.htm.

7. Honnold, RoseMary. "See YA Around: Summer Reading Program 2002 Links." www.cplrmh.com/SRP2002.html.

8. Discovery School. "Puzzlemaker." http://puzzlemaker.school.discovery.com.

FOR SPICES AND HERBS:

1. JT Software. "Bingomaker." www.jtsoftware.com/demohelp.html.

2. Spice Advice. "Spice Encyclopedia." www.spiceadvice.com.

3. Culinary Café. "Spices and Herbs." www.culinarycafe.com/Spices_Herbs/index.html.

4. American Spice Trade Association. "The Spices of Antiquity." www.astaspice.org/history/history_01.htm.

FOR CHOCOLATE:

1. Adoff, Arnold. 1989. *Chocolate Dreams*. New York: Lothrop, Lee and Shepard Books.

2. Allenbaugh, Kay, comp. 1999. *Chocolate for a Woman's Soul*. New York: Simon and Schuster.

3. Burford, Betty. 1994. *Chocolate by Hershey*. Minneapolis: Carolrhoda Books.

4. Coe, Sophie D., and Michael D. Coe. 1996. *The True History of Chocolate*. New York: Thames and Hudson.

5. Dineen, Jacqueline. 1991. *Chocolate*. Minneapolis: Carolrhoda Books.

6. *Hershey's 1934 Cookbook*, rev. 1993. New York: Smithmark.

7. Howe, James.1990. *Hot Fudge*. New York: Morrow Junior Books.

8. Groom, Winston. *Forrest Gump: My Favorite Chocolate Recipes: Mama's Fudge, Cookies, Cakes, and Candies*. 1995. Birmingham: Oxmoor House.

9. "Famous Poems (Mis)Remembered by Peter Mansbach." http://hometown.aol.com/pmansbach/choc.html.

10. Virtual Chocolate's Quotes www.virtualchocolate.com/quotes.cfm.

11. Waller, Kathleen. "Chocolate Trivia." Waller Design. http://home.earthlink.net/~wallerdesign/trivia.html.

FOR BASEBALL:

1. Garber, Angus G. 1988. *Baseball Legends: The Greatest Players, Best Games, and Magical Moments: Then and Now.* New York: Gallery.

2. Italia, Bob. 1990. *Baseball Legends.* Bloomington, MN: Abdo and Daughters.

3. Morrison, Lillian, comp. 1992. *At the Crack of the Bat: Baseball Poems.* New York: Hyperion Books for Children.

4. Obojski, Robert. 1989. *Baseball Bloopers and Other Curious Incidents.* New York: Sterling.

5. Thayer, Ernest Lawrence. 1968. *Casey at the Bat.* Englewood Cliffs, NJ: Prentice.

6. The Baseball Archive. "History." www.baseball1.com/c-history.html.

7. "The History of Baseball in the 19th Century. www.geocities.com/Colosseum/Bleachers/5573.

FOR READERS THEATER:

1. Barchers, Suzanne I. 1997. *Fifty Fabulous Fables: Beginning Readers Theatre.* Englewood, CO: Teacher Ideas Press.

2. Barchers, Suzanne I. 1993. *Readers Theatre for Beginning Readers.* Englewood, CO: Teacher Ideas Press.

3. Barchers, Suzanne I. 1994. *Scary Readers Theatre.* Englewood, CO: Teacher Ideas Press.

4. Bauer, Caroline Feller. 1987. *Presenting Readers Theater.* New York: H.W. Wilson.

5. Fleischman, Paul. 2000. *Big Talk: Poems for Four Voices.* Cambridge: Candlewick Press.

6. Fredericks, Anthony D. 1993. *Frantic Frogs and Other Frankly Fractured Folktales for Readers Theatre.* Englewood, CO: Teacher Ideas Press.

7. Shepard, Aaron. "Alan Shepard's RT Page: Scripts and Tips for Reader's Theater." http://aaronshep.com/rt.

APPENDIX A: THE QUESTIONNAIRE

The libraries that responded to our listserv posts and e-mails received the following questionnaire:

Greetings!

You are receiving this questionnaire because your library Web site or your e-mail to me indicated that you have programming geared towards senior adults. The information I collect from these questionnaires will be used in a new book about programs and services for senior adults to be published by Neal-Schuman Publishers, Inc. in 2003. I hope this book will be a valuable tool for the libraries already providing programming for this user group and will be an inspiration to other libraries to begin doing so. Please mail, e-mail, or fax your answers to me by December 30.

PART ONE: YOUR LIBRARY

1. Does your library have a department and/or staff devoted to senior adult service and programs?

   If yes, list number of staff and the title of the department/staff.

   If no, who plans and implements the programs/services?

2. Library size: what is your annual circulation and service population? Please share any senior demographic data from your area that you may use when planning programs.

PART TWO: OUTREACH

3. Do you offer homebound service? How many staff members are involved? Do you use any volunteers for this service? How many homebound patrons do you serve per month? How often do you visit a patron?

4. Do you serve nursing homes? If yes, do you offer programs? How often? Book deposits? Individual visits?

5. Do you serve assisted living facilities? If yes, do you offer programs? How often? Book deposits? Individual visits?

PART THREE: IN THE LIBRARY

6. Do you have any special collections for senior adults? Large Print? Audio or talking books? BiFolkal or theme kits? Special equipment? Other?

7. Do you offer computer classes just for senior adults? If yes, do you have a class outline you would like to share? Do you have handouts you would like to share?

8. Do you offer programs just for senior adults? If yes, what are your most popular/appreciated programs? Tell us about them: title, brief description, length, special materials, speakers, number of staff involved, costs. Any feedback from the audience?

9. Do you offer intergenerational programs that involve seniors? If yes, what are your most popular/appreciated programs? Tell us about them: title, brief description, length, special materials, speakers, number of staff involved, costs. Any feedback from the audience?

PART FOUR: SHARE YOUR EXPERIENCE

10. Do you have any suggestions, tips, bits of wisdom, and experience that you would like to share with other libraries that want to start programming for seniors? Do you have favorite resources for your programs?

Your contributions will be acknowledged in our senior adults services book. Please provide contact information with your reply: your name, title, name of library, address, phone, fax, and e-mail.

Thank you for sharing your work with other libraries!

RoseMary Honnold
Coshocton Public Library
655 Main ST
Coshocton, OH 43812
Phone 740-622-0956 ext 14
honnolro@oplin.org
Fax 740-622-4331

APPENDIX B:
OUR CONTRIBUTERS

Many thanks go to the following librarians and libraries that shared their services, programs, Web sites, tips, and experiences in serving senior adults:

Alachua County Library District
Gainesville, FL
2001 Annual Circulation: 2,500,000+
Contact: Carol Hole

Alameda County Library
Fremont, CA
2001 Annual Circulation: 3,995,997
Contact: Richard Bray

Allen County Public Library
Ft. Wayne, IN
2001 Annual Circulation: unreported
Contact: Peg Heinze

Bemis Public Library
Littleton, CO
2001 Annual Circulation: 340,000
Contact: Jan A. Knauer

Bethel Park Public Library
Bethel Park, PA
2001 Annual Circulation: 280,000
Contact: Mary Mullen

Birchard Public Library of Sandusky County
Fremont, OH
2001 Annual Circulation: unreported
Contact: Nancy Koebel

Boonslick Regional Library: Sedalia Branch
Sedalia, MO
2001 Annual Circulation: 114,906
Contact: Jackie Oliphant

Champaign County Library
Urbana, OH
2001 Annual Circulation: unreported
Contact: Gloria Malone

Coshocton Public Library
Coshocton, OH
2002 Annual Circulation: 529,429
Contact: RoseMary Honnold and Saralyn Mesaros

Dallas Public Library
Dallas, TX

Delaware County District Library
Delaware, OH
2001 Annual Circulation: 294,829
Contact: Deborah Malecha

Delta Township District Library
Lansing, MI
2001 Annual Circulation: unreported
Contact: Mary Rzepczynski

El Paso Public Library
El Paso, TX
2001 Annual Circulation: 2,274,978
Contact: Mary Helen Michals

Fairport Public Library
Fairport, NY
2001 Annual Circulation: unreported
Contact: Margaret Pilaroscia

Flesh Public Library
Piqua, OH
2001 Annual Circulation: unreported
Contact: Rachelle Ramsey

Fruitville Library
Sarasota, FL
2001 Annual Circulation: 262,712
Contact: Alexce Douville

Gates Public Library
Rochester, NY
2001 Annual Circulation: 403,042
Contact: Heidi Jung

Greene County Public Library
Xenia, OH
2001 Annual Circulation: 2,073,000
Contact: Martha Gardin

Hamilton Public Library
Hamilton, Ontario
Contact: Kathy Denomy

Haverhill Public Library
Haverhill, MA
2001 Annual Circulation: 426,000
Contact: Vicki Murphy

Hennepin County Library
Minnetonka, MN
2001 Annual Circulation: 10,000,000
Contact: Patrick Jones

Henry County Library
Clinton, MO
2001 Annual Circulation: 129,106
Contact: Debbie Jones and Liz Cashell

Houston Public Library
Houston, TX

Jefferson County Library Northwest Branch
High Ridge, MO
2001 Annual Circulation: 225,374
Contact: Susie Davis

Jefferson County Public Library
Lakewood, CO
2001 Annual Circulation: 3,170,000
Contact: Terri Bailey

Lake County Library System
FL 2001 Annual Circulation: unreported
Contact: Wendy Breeden

Lawrence Public Library
Lawrence, KS
2001 Annual Circulation: 435,000
Contact: Pattie Johnston

Lorain Public Library System
Lorain, OH
2001 Annual Circulation: 1,489,972
Contact: Valerie Smith

Los Angeles Public Library
Los Angeles, CA
2001 Annual Circulation: 13,000,000+
Contact: Maureen Wade

Loudon County Public Library
Loudon County, VA
2001 Annual Circulation: unreported
Contact: Linda Holtslander and Maria McClintock

Loudonville Public Library
Loudonville, OH
2001 Annual Circulation: unreported
Contact: Joy Zemrock

Marathon County Public Library
Wausau, WI
2001 Annual Circulation: 769,000
Contact: Barbara Ritchie

Marion Baysinger Memorial County Library
Groveland, FL
2001 Annual Circulation: unreported
Contact: Kristen Wiley

Mid-Continent Public Library
Clay, Jackson, and Platte Counties, MO
2001 Annual Circulation: unreported
Contact: Marlena Boggs

Middendorf-Kredell Branch Library
O'Fallon, MO
2001 Annual Circulation: unreported
Contact: Lisa Lucido

Middle Country Public Library
Centereach, NY
2001 Annual Circulation: unreported
Contact: Illena Betcher

Missouri State Library
Jefferson City, MO
2001 Annual Circulation: unreported
Contact: Nancee Dahms-Stinson

Muskingum County Library System
Zanesville, OH
2001 Annual Circulation: 753,000
Contact: Cherie Bronkar

North Canton Public Library
North Canton, OH
2002 Annual Circulation: 905,000
Contact: Linda Bayman

North Miami Public Library
North Miami, FL
2001 Annual Circulation: 101,600
Contact: Ilene Zaleski

Orange County Library System
Orlando, FL
2001 Annual Circulation: unreported
Contact: Gail Carroll

Peterborough Town Library
Peterborough, NH
2001 Annual Circulation: 80,000
Contact: Charlotte Rabbitt

Plain City Public Library
Plain City, OH
2001 Annual Circulation: unreported
Contact: Chris Long

Richmond Public Library
Richmond, BC
2001 Annual Circulation: 3,305,044
Contact: Desiree Baron

Savannah Library
Savannah, MO
2001 Annual Circulation: 110,000
Contact: Connie Rehm

State Library of Florida
Contact: Cay Hohmeister

Texas State Library and Archives Commission
Talking Book Program of Texas
Austin, TX
2001 Annual Circulation: 800,000+
Contact: Ava M. Smith

Tiffin-Seneca Public Library
Tiffin, OH
2001 Annual Circulation: 428,561
Contact: June Huss

Toronto Public Library
Toronto, Ontario
2001 Annual Circulation: 27,700,000
Contact: Arlene Chan, Susan Back

Tuscarawas County Public Library
New Philadelphia, OH
2001 Annual Circulation: 625,069
Contact: Bobbi Deakyne

Way Library
Perrysburg, OH
2001 Annual Circulation: unreported
Contact: unreported

West Palm Beach Public Library
West Palm Beach, FL
2001 Annual Circulation: unreported
Contact: Barbara J. Storch

APPENDIX C:
THE WISDOM OF
YOUR COLLEAGUES

By three methods we may learn wisdom:
First, by reflection, which is noblest;
Second, by imitation, which is easiest;
and third by experience, which is the bitterest.

—Confucius

OVERVIEW

Many of our questionnaire respondents included tips and advice they found to be helpful for serving senior adults. This appendix is a compilation of their insightful comments and their knowledge gained by experience. We hope you will find guidance, ideas, and support from their expertise.

ADVICE FROM OUR CONTRIBUTORS

FROM RICHARD BRAY OF ALMEDA COUNTY LIBRARY IN FREMONT, CA:

Seniors are first and foremost people! Lots of nonseniors don't get this; either they have little or no experience, stereotypes, lack of awareness, etc. We spend lots of time educating our senior service representatives, (who also have seventeen other hats, as do most library staff), our branch managers, front-line staff of all stripes, and ourselves.

FROM PEG HEINZE OF ALLEN COUNTY PUBLIC LIBRARY IN FT. WAYNE, IN:

I have found that there are still people who think seniors only read the small meaningless romances or westerns. They have yet to grasp the fact that seniors in our community are very knowledgeable of the current books and want them as quick as all our patrons that can walk through the door at our main library or the branches. Many times they ask for a book before I have heard of it and I add my name to the hold list after them! I like to think of the seniors as my grandparents, as mine passed away years ago. This way I know I am giving them the respect they deserve and I am not treating them as I would a child. I love to hear their stories, so the remembering programs we do really bring those out. Everyone likes to talk about themselves and about their memories. These folks know me well after twenty years and my children grew up in the stories that I have told them. These are my friends.

FROM JAN A. KNAUER OF BEMIS PUBLIC LIBRARY IN LITTLETON, CO:

Find out where seniors get their information and news. Is there a senior center? Are there publications aimed at seniors? Who are the community members already working with seniors? Are there Web groups? Special programs at medical centers or Free Universities and Community Colleges? Would groups let you come in and speak, booktalk, or read stories?

FROM DEBORAH MALECHA OF DELAWARE COUNTY DISTRICT LIBRARY IN DELAWARE, OH:

Show them how to adjust the computers so they can see the text and graphics. Speak slowly, assume nobody's hearing is really good, and *be patient.* I also teach keyboard shortcuts—older hands have a hard time with a mouse.

FROM BARBARA GROFF OF GREEN COUNTY PUBLIC LIBRARY IN XENIA, OH:

The Outreach Department works closely with the Activity Coordinators of senior care facilities. We make it a point to keep plenty of program materials. Favorite resources include the BiFolkal kits and Sing-Along videos.

FROM VICKI MURPHY OF HAVERHILL PUBLIC LIBRARY IN HAVERHILL, MA:

The best bit of advice is to be patient with this group and get to know what they are interested in learning about and discussing. They have so much wisdom to offer and are deeply grateful for library extension services. Every library should reach out to the elderly.

FROM CAROL HOLE OF ALACHUA COUNTY LIBRARY DISTRICT IN GAINESVILLE, FL:

I consider it very important not to condescend to seniors—they hate that! And it's very important to put deposit collections on wheels—otherwise they get dumped in the activities room and many residents who can't get to the activities room can't get to them.

FROM KATHY DENOMY OF HAMILTON PUBLIC LIBRARY IN HAMILTON, ONTARIO:

I once organized a staff training workshop entitled "Through Older Eyes" about the challenges and pleasures of working with seniors. I motivated the audience by reviewing our changing demographics—the aging population phenomena. I contacted a government official who worked with me and supplied yellow tinted glasses, gloves, leg weights, wrist weights, ear plugs, and other things that mocked the effects of aging on the human body. Everyone had to assume a "handicap" and then was given a common library task to accomplish. Staff found it very enlightening and had fun at the same time. I then reviewed library materials and services most popular with seniors and how to make them more accessible. We also had a discussion period. At that time I had already been working with seniors for a number of years so I was able to share some funny (and endearing) anecdotes. The goal was to instill confidence, empathy, and enthusiasm when dealing with older persons.

FROM PATTIE JOHNSTON OF LAWRENCE PUBLIC LIBRARY IN LAWRENCE, MO:

I would suggest that part of the training be visits to local senior resident centers. Many people have not been inside a nursing facility, but many have not seen the retirement centers that provide independent and/or assisted living, either. This can dispel certain perceptions. Knowing how the buildings are arranged and how the residences are administered are a big help in planning programs. Becoming acquainted with the activity directors or resident services administrators can make a big difference in how your programs are attended or advertised, also. Generally, the ADs and RSAs welcome teaming up with other agencies to provide programs. Becoming knowledgeable about the programs and events being held at these facilities can give you ideas for programs and also prevent conflicts in planning. Perhaps inviting activity directors to talk to your staff would be enlightening, too.

FROM LINDA BAYMAN OF NORTH CANTON PUBLIC LIBRARY IN NORTH CANTON, OH:

Before I worked in libraries, I spent several years as an Activities Director at a nursing home. The people at the nursing home ranged from totally oriented and interested to totally disoriented. Therefore, it was necessary to do several levels of programming for each group. It's possible to do a program on the same topic for each level but you have to be careful not to mix your audiences.

For instance, you can do a nostalgic book talk about *Remembering Woolworth's* for oriented and independent seniors and they'll probably enjoy it. You can even bring in some pictures of ads or other memorabilia from Woolworth's. But think twice before you do a BiFolkal Kit on Woolworth's (or shopping five and dimes) for this group, because they don't need the visual, olfactory, or auditory clues to remember, and may be offended that you chose to use them. Nursing homes or adult day cares, on the other hand, might not be the place to do a full blown book-talk about Woolworth's, because the people may need a little more help with remembering. They might also be bored with too much reading (but would enjoy the photos). This would be the place for a BiFolkal Kit.

FROM SUSIE DAVIS OF JEFFERSON COUNTY LIBRARY IN HIGH RIDGE, MO:

Seniors do not fit into a neat little box. They are not interested in the things we think they are. They like fun and interesting things and sharing their experiences.

FROM PATTIE JOHNSTON OF LAWRENCE PUBLIC LIBRARY IN LAWRENCE, KS:

Take the programs to the focused audience instead of always expecting the audience to come to you. A variety of topics should be presented. Join the area senior groups, i.e. AARP, local Council on Aging, to gain an idea of the issues that are of concern to older adults. Make yourself and the library known to local agencies that work with older adults. Gather brochures, pamphlets, and booklets that can be given to let your patrons know of the services and options available in your community. Realize that not all of your programs will be successful. Have a booth at local health fairs, work with agencies to plan workshops. Work with activity directors to combine efforts. Focus on an age group. Fifty-year-olds are not the same as seventy-year-olds. Be realistic in expectations. Activity levels, health and mental status, weather, time of day or day of the week. Sunday afternoon is a good time. Know your community. Don't duplicate services. Warehouse information about the services available; if you didn't know about it, your patrons probably don't either.

FROM CHERIE BRONKAR OF MUSKINGUM COUNTY LIBRARY SYSTEM IN ZANESVILLE, OH:

Try to make the programs appropriate to your group (Nursing home as opposed to assisted living). Start out with some pretty easy activities; each facility is different and you will get a feel for what they want after the first visit. Ask for their input on what they would like you to do. Use lots of humor. Funny stories, poems, quips—all the groups love to laugh and this is a great way to get them interested in what you are doing. I always hand out wordfinds at every program. All the groups love to get them even the ones you wouldn't think would be able to do them can surprise you. Use food! Can't stress that enough. It doesn't have to be elaborate. Use taste, touch, and smell to stimulate their senses.

FROM CHARLOTTE RABBITT OF PETERBOROUGH TOWN LIBRARY IN NH:

Like any library program, the people who benefit from it are usually very appreciative. Programs sometimes take time to catch on.

FROM DESIREE BARON OF RICHMOND PUBLIC LIBRARY IN RICHMOND, BC CANADA:

I draw my inspiration for senior programs from things that I see in the local paper and local senior papers.

FROM CONNIE REHM OF SAVANNAH LIBRARY IN SAVANNAH, MO:

Keep your ears open! What are people interested in? Is someone in your community involved in a unique activity? Keep things "short and sweet." Ask folks to call and commit themselves to attending.

FROM AVA M. SMITH OF TEXAS STATE LIBRARY IN AUSTIN, TX:

Pay attention to the content of both programming and collection development. Senior adults generally are well-read, are voracious readers, and are eager for new experiences and knowledge. At the same time, their reading tastes generally are conservative, and they find excessive language, violence, and sexual content to be distasteful. Genre fiction is very popular, particularly romances and westerns.

FROM JUNE HUSS OF TIFFIN-SENECA PUBLIC LIBRARY IN TIFFIN, OH:

The individual assigned to present programs must genuinely CARE about older adults and have the DESIRE to entertain them. A good working relationship is essential with other library staff members. Helpful also is a good relationship with the local newspaper and radio station. Cooperate with the facilities' activity directors and staff. Ask them for program topics of special interest to their residents. Plan programs well in advance. Visual aids improve recall for all adults. Be flexible with your programs. Depending on population served, I may change some portions of my presentations to fit the interests of nursing homes, assisted living, or independent living facilities. I very rarely used "canned" programs. My programs are unique—researched and developed personally with help from library reference staff when needed.

APPENDIX D: ELECTRONIC RESOURCES

ALA AND CLA WEB SITES FOR SENIOR SERVICES

1. American Library Association. "Outreach Resources to Underserved Populations: Services to the Elderly." www.ala.org/Content/Navigation Menu/Our_Association/Offices/Literacy_and_Outr each_Services/Outreach_Resources/Services_to_El derly_People.htm.

2. American Library Association. "Guidelines to Library Services to Older Adults." www.ala.org/ Content/NavigationMenu/Our_Association/Offices/ Literacy_and_Outreach_Services/Outreach_Resour ces/elderly.pdf.

3. Canadian Library Association. "Canadian Guidelines on Library and Information Services for Older Adults." www.cla.ca/about/olderadults.htm.

ELECTRONIC DISCUSSION LISTS

Discussion lists are a great way to make connections with other librarians working with seniors. Share ideas, ask questions, find resources, share problems and concerns, and make friends!

1. SeniorLib is a discussion list for librarians serving senior adults started by the authors of *Serving Seniors: a How-To-Do-It Manual for Librarians*.

Topics include Homebound Service, nursing home and assisted living programming, programming in libraries for the senior adult audience, collection development, and programming materials. To subscribe: send an e-mail to SeniorLib-subscribe@topica.com. To post: SeniorLib@topica.com.

2. SeniorServ, sponsored by the ALA RUSA Committee on Library Services to an Aging Population, is a discussion list for the purpose of sharing information about library services to senior adults. To subscribe: send an e-mail to listproc@ala.org , leave the subject line blank, and send the following message: subscribe SeniorServ YourFirstName YourLastName To post: SeniorServ@ala.org.

PUBLIC LIBRARY SENIOR WEB SITES

Many libraries are creating special pages on their Web sites for senior adults. Several examples of Web sites are listed below to give you ideas for creating one for your library's Web site.

1. Allan County Public Library Outreach Services. www.acpl.lib.in.us/outreach_services/index.html.

2. Bethlehem Public Library, Delmar, NY. www.uhls.org/bethlehem/weblinks.asp?detail=Senior%20Resources&source=a.

3. Boston Public Library. "Services to Senior Adults." www.bpl.org/central/adult/senior.htm.

4. Brunswick Community Library. "Sites for Seniors Page." www.brunswicklibrary.org/SeniorSites.html.

5. Dallas Public Library. "Growing On: Library Resources for Adults 50+." http://dallaslibrary.org/ss/seniors.htm.

6. El Paso Public Library. "El Paso Public Library Seniors Page." www.ci.el-paso.tx.us/library/epplsp.htm.

7. Hammond Public Library. "Senior Connection." www.hammond.lib.in.us/seniormenu.htm.

8. Hennepin County Public Library. "Senior Links." www.hclib.org/seniorlinks.

9. Houston Public Library. "Services for Persons with Disabilities." www.hpl.lib.tx.us/hpl/disabled.html.

10. Lexington Public Library. "Outreach Services." www.lexpublib.org/outreach/index.cfm.

11. Loudon County Public Library. "Outreach Services." www.lcpl.lib.va.us/outreach.htm.

12. Public Library District of Columbia. "Events at the Martin Luther King Jr. Memorial Library." http://dclibrary.org/calendar/thismonth.mlk.html#seniors.

13. Portland State University's (PSU) Senior Adults Learning Center (SALC). http://web.pdx.edu/~psu01435/salc.html.

14. Queens Borough Public Library. "Programs and Services For Older Adults." www.queenslibrary.org/programs/special/index.asp?special=older.

15. Teton County Public Library. "Adult Programs." http://tclib.org/adults/index.html.

16. Texas State Library and Archives Commission. "Talking Book Program." www.TexastalkingBooks.org.

APPENDIX E: BOOKLISTS FOR SENIOR PROGRAMMING

OVERVIEW

This collection of booklists will be useful when developing story times, programs, collection development and booklists to handout to seniors, grandparents and activity directors.

STORY BOOKS FOR READ-ALOUDS

Compiled by June Hess of Tiffin-Seneca Public Library

1. Calmenson, Stephanie. 1994. *Rosie, a Visiting Dog's Story*. New York: Clarion Books.

2. Ernst, Lisa Campbell. 1983. *Sam Johnson and the Blue Ribbon Quilt*. New York: Lothrop, Lee and Shepard Books.

3. Fox, Mem. 1989. *Wilfrid Gordon McDonald Partridge*. Brooklyn, New York: Kane/Miller Book.

4. Houston, Gloria. 1992. *My Great-Aunt Arizona*. New York: HarperCollins.

5. Leaf, Munro. 1964. *Story of Ferdinand*. New York: The Viking Press.

6. Lionni, Leo. 1964. *Tico and the Golden Wings*. New York: Pantheon Books.

7. Romanova, Natalia. 1985. *Once There Was a Tree*. New York: Dial Books.

8. Roop, Peter. 1985. *Keep the Lights Burning, Abbie*. Minneapolis: Carolrhoda Books.

9. Silverstein, Shel. 1999. *The Giving Tree*. New York: HarperCollins.

10. Vaughan, Marcia K. 1986. *Wombat Stew.* Englewood Cliffs, NJ.: Silver Burdett.

11. Viorst, Judith. 1972. *Alexander & the Terrible, Horrible, No Good, Very Bad Day.* New York: Atheneum.

PICTURE BOOKS ADULTS ENJOY

Compiled by Shirley McDougal of Medina County District Library

1. Andrews, Jan. 1991. *The Auction.* New York: Macmillan.

2. Brown, Ruth. 1996. *The Ghost of Greyfriar's Bobby.* New York: Dutton Children's Books.

3. Buehner, Caralyn. 1996. *Fanny's Dream.* New York: Dial Books for Young Readers.

4. Bunting, Eve. 1990. *The Wall.* New York: Clarion Books.

5. Foreman, Michael. 1993. *War Game.* New York: Arcade.

6. Hopkinson, Deborah. 1993. *Sweet Clara and the Freedom Quilt.* New York: Knopf.

7. Innocenti, Roberto. 1996. *Rose Blanche.* San Diego: Creative Editions/Harcourt Brace.

8. MacLachlan, Patricia. 1994. *All the Places to Love.* New York: HarperCollins.

9. MacLachlan, Patricia. 1995. *What You Know First.* New York: HarperCollins.

10. McKissack, Pat. 1994. *Christmas in the Big House, Christmas in the Quarters.* New York: Scholastic.

11. Mochizuki, Ken. 1993. *Baseball Saved Us.* New York: Lee & Low.

12. Polacco, Patricia. 1992. *Chicken Sunday.* New York: Philomel Books.

13. Polacco, Patricia. 1990. *Just Plain Fancy.* New York: Bantam Books.

14. Polacco, Patricia. 1994. *Pink and Say.* New York: Philomel Books.

15. Sanders, Scott. 1992. *Warm as Wool.* New York: Bradbury Press.

16. Shannon, George. 1993. *Climbing Kansas Mountains*. New York: Bradbury Press.

17. Tsuchiya, Yukio. 1988. *The Faithful Elephants*. Boston: Houghton Mifflin.

18. Whelan, Gloria. 1992. *Bringing the Farmhouse Home*. New York: Simon & Schuster Books for Young Readers.

19. Wilde, Oscar. 1984. *The Selfish Giant*. New York: Scholastic.

PICTURE BOOKS SENIORS ENJOY

Complied by Laura Krentz and Joni Kreuser and of Hennepin County Public Library.

1. Cooney, Barbara. 1982. *Miss Rumphius*. New York: Viking Press.

2. Hickcox, Ruth. 1998. *Great-Grandmother's Treasure*. New York: Dial Books for Young Readers.

3. Houston, Gloria. 1988. *The Year of the Perfect Christmas Tree*. New York: Dial Books for Young Readers.

4. Lunge-Larsen, Lise. 2001. *The Race of the Birkebeiners*. New York: Houghton Mifflin.

5. McKissack, Patricia. 1997. *Ma Dear's Aprons*. New York: Atheneum Books for Young Readers.

6. Polacco, Patricia. 1999. *Welcome Comfort*. New York: Philomel Books.

7. Rahaman, Vashanti. 1997. *Read for Me, Mama*. Honesdale, PA: Boyds Mills Press.

8. Wojciechowski, Susan. 1995. *The Christmas Miracle of Jonathan Toomey*. Cambridge: Candlewick Press.

CHILDREN'S CHAPTER BOOKS SENIORS ENJOY

Compiled by Laura Krentz and Joni Kreuser and of Hennepin County Public Library

1. DiCamillo, Kate. 2000. *Because of Winn-Dixie*. Cambridge: Candlewick Press.

2. Fletcher, Ralph J. 1995. *Fig Pudding*. New York: Clarion Books.

3. Haseley, Dennis. 2002. *The Amazing Thinking Machine*. New York: Dial Books.

4. Hill, Kirkpatrick. 2000. *The Year of Miss Agnes*. New York: Margaret K. McElderry Books.

5. Horvath, Polly. 1999. *The Trolls*. New York: Farrar Strouse Giroux.

6. Kinsey-Warnock, Natalie. 1989. *The Canada Geese Quilt*. New York: Cobblehill Books/Dutton.

7. Lawrence, Iain. 2001. *Lord of the Nutcracker Men*. New York: Delacorte Press.

8. Peck, Richard. 2001. *Fair Weather*. New York: Dial Books.

9. Peck, Richard. 1998. *A Long Way From Chicago*. New York: Dial Books for Young Readers.

10. Peck, Richard. 2000. *A Year Down Yonder*. New York: Dial Books for Young Readers.

RECOMMENDED FOR READING ALOUD PROGRAMS

Compiled by Barbara Gillespie, Medina County District Library and Peggy Holley and Paul Ward of Portsmouth Public Library

1. Beno, Mike, ed. 1998. *Forks in the Road*. Greendale, WI: Reminisce Books.

2. Beno, Mike, ed. 1996. *Christmases We Used to Know*. Greendale, WI: Reminisce Books.

3. Beno, Mike, ed. 1999. *When the Banks Close, We Opened Our Hearts*. Greendale, WI: R.J. Reiman.

4. Bloom, Harold, ed. 1998. *The Best of the Best American Poetry 1988–1997*. New York: Scribner Poetry.

5. Bombeck, Erma. 1991. *When You Look Like Your Passport Photo, It's Time to Go Home*. New York: HarperCollins.

6. Brokaw, Tom. 1999. *The Greatest Generation Speaks*. New York: Random House.

7. Browning, Elizabeth Barrett. *(Anything)*

8. Burns, George. 1996. *100 Years, 100 Stories.* New York: G.P. Putnam's.

9. Cunningham, Michael. 2000. *Crowns: Portraits of Black Women in Church Hats.* New York: Doubleday.

10. Dregni, Michael, ed. 1999. *This Old Farm: a Treasury of Family Farm Memories.* Stillwater, MN: Voyageur Press.

11. Foley, Martha, ed. 1952. *The Best of the Best Short Stories 1915–50.* Boston: Houghton Mifflin.

12. Frost, Robert. 1979. "The Mending Wall" and "Birches." *The Poetry of Robert Frost.* Ed. Edward Connery Lathem.). New York: H. Holt.

13. Fulgham, Robert. 1997. *True Love: Stories Told to and by Robert Fulgham.* New York: HarperCollins.

14. Halberstam, Davis, ed. 1999. T*he Best American Sports Writing of the Century.* Boston: Houghton Mifflin.

15. *Life in the Slow Lane: Tales of Covered Bridges Written by and for the People Who Love 'Em.* 1998. Greendale, WI: Reiman.

16. Mohr, Nicholasa. 1995. *The Song of El Coqui and Other Tales of Puerto Rico.* New York: Viking/Penguin Group.

17. Mulvey, Deb, ed. 1995. *"We Had Everything But Money."* New Jersey: Crescent Books.

18. Rooney, Andy. *(Anything)*

19. Rubin, Robert Alden, ed. 1993. *Poetry Out Loud.* Chapel Hill: Algonquin Books of Chapel Hill.

20. Singer, Isaac Bashevis. *(Anything)*

21. Stolley, Richard B., ed. 2000. *Life Century of Change: America in Pictures 1900–2000.* Boston: Bulfinch Press.

22. Stuart, Jesse. 1963. *A Jesse Stuart Reader: stories and poems.* New York: McGraw-Hill.

23. Sword, Elmer Bernard. 1965. *The Story of Portsmouth.* Portsmouth, OH: Compton Engraving and Printing.

24. Thurber, James. *(Anything)*

25. Yolen, Jane, ed. 1986. *Favorite Folktales from Around the World*. New York: Pantheon Books.
26. Zurcher, Neil. *Neil Zurker's One Tank Trips*. Cleveland, Ohio: WJW-TV8.

RECOMMENDED TITLES FOR READ-ALOUD PROGRAMS

Compiled by Jenny Cowling of Vern Riffe Library.

1. Devlin, Wende and Harry. 1980. *Cranberry Thanksgiving*. New York: Four Winds Press.
2. Gross, Ruth Belov. 1974. *The Bremen Town Musicians*. New York: Scholastic Book Services.
3. Hazeltine, Alice Isabel. 1947. *The Easter Book of Legends and Stories*. New York: Lothrop, Lee & Shepard.
4. Henry, O. 1984. *The Gift of the Magi*. Mankato, MN: Creative Education.
5. Joseph, Jim. 1997. *Heroes and Other Folks*. Huntington, WV: University Editions.
6. Le Sueur, Meridel. 1947. *Little Brother of the Wilderness: The Story of Johnny Appleseed*. New York: A.A. Knopf.
7. Lenski, Lois. 1945. *The Strawberry Girl*. Philadelphia: Lippincott.
8. Robinson, Barbara. 1972. *The Best Christmas Pageant Ever*. New York: Harper & Row.

READ-ALOUDS

Compiled by the Missouri State Library.

1. Banks, Carolyn, and Janis Rizzo, eds. 1992. *A Loving Voice: A Caregiver's Book of Read-Aloud Stories for the Elderly*. Philadelphia: Charles Press.
2. Gardner, Martin, ed. 1995. *Famous Poems from Bygone Days*. New York, NY: Dover Publications.
3. Ward, Jerry W., Jr., ed. 1997. *Trouble the Water: 250 Years of African-American Poetry*. New York, NY: Penguin.

READ-ALOUD LISTS ON THE WEB

1. Rokicki, Melissa, comp. "Books to Read Aloud to Adults." www.webrary.org/rs/flbklists/Aloud.html.

GRANDPARENTS RAISING GRANDCHILDREN FICTION BOOKLIST

Compiled by Suzy Murray of Sacramento Public Library on YALSA-BK discussion list.

1. Bauer, Joan. 2000. *Rules of the Road.* New York: Puffin Books.

2. Bauer, Joan. 2002. *Stand Tall.* New York: G.P. Putnam's Sons.

3. Bawden, Nina. 1998. *Granny the Pag.* New York: Puffin Books.

4. Carter, Forrest. 1976. *The Education of Little Tree.* New York: Delacorte Press.

5. Chambers, Veronica. 1998. *Marisol and Magdalena: The Sound of Our Sisterhood.* New York: Jump at the Sun.

6. Creech, Sharon. 1994. *Walk Two Moons.* New York: HarperCollins.

7. Davis, Jenny. 1991. *Checking on the Moon.* New York: Orchard Books.

8. Dorris, Michael. 1987. *Yellow Raft in Blue Water.* New York: H. Holt.

9. Gonzales, Albino. 2001. *No Lack of Lonesome.* Grand Junction, CO: Farolito Press.

10. Grover, Laurie Ann. 2002. *Loose Threads.* New York: Margaret K. McElderry Books.

11. Hamilton, Virginia. 1984. *A Little Love.* New York: Philomel Books.

12. Henkes, Kevin. 1992. *Words of Stone.* New York: Greenwillow Books.

13. Hernandez, Irene Beltran. 2000. *Woman Soldier.* Waco, Texas: Blue Rose Books.

14. Johnson, Angela. 1993. *Toning the Sweep.* New York: Orchard Books.

15. Lachtman, Ofelia Dumas. 1997. *Call Me Consuelo.* Houston: Piñata Books.

16. Lynch, Chris. 2001. *Freewill.* New York: HarperCollins.

17. Mosher, Richard. 2001. *Zazoo.* New York: Clarion Books.

18. Nolan, Han. 1997. *Dancing on the Edge.* San Diego: Harcourt Brace.

19. Paterson, Katherine. 2002. *The Same Stuff as Stars.* New York: Houghton Mifflin.

20. Peck, Richard. 1998. *Strays Like Us.* New York: Dial Books.

21. Philbrick, W.R. 1993. *Freak the Mighty.* New York: Blue Sky Press.

22. Van Draanen, Wendelin. *Sammy Keyes*series. 23. Voigt, Cynthia. 1983. *Homecoming.* New York: Atheneum.

23. Voigt, Cynthia. 1983. *Homecoming.* New York: Atheneum.

24. White, Ruth. 1996. *Belle Prater's Boy.* New York: Farrer Straus Giroux.

25. Yep, Laurence. 1977. *Child of the Owl.* New York: Harper & Row.

GRANDPARENT PICTURE BOOKS LIST

1. Bahr, Mary. 1992. *The Memory Box.* Morton Grove, IL: A. Whitman.

2. Ballard, Robin. 1992. *Granny and Me.* New York: Greenwillow Books.

3. Beil, Karen Magnuson. 1992. *Grandma According to Me.* New York: Delacorte Press.

4. Buckley, Helen E. 1994. *Grandfather and I.* New York: Lothrop Lee & Shepard.

5. Butterworth, Nick. 1992. *My Grandpa is Amazing.* Cambridge, MA: Candelwick Press.

6. Caseley, Judith. 1990. *Grandpa's Garden Lunch.* New York: Greenwillow Books.

7. Compton, Kenn and Joanne. 1993. *Granny Greenteeth and the Noise in the Night.* New York: Holiday House.

8. Darling, Benjamin. 1992. *Valerie and the Silver Pear.* New York: Four Winds Press.

9. DeFelice, Cynthia. 1992. *When Grandpa Kissed His Elbow.* New York: Macmillan.

10. Drucker, Malka. 1992. *Grandma's Latkes.* San Diego: Harcourt Brace Jovanovich.

11. Foreman, Michael. 1994. *Grandfather's Pencil and the Room of Stories.* San Diego: Harcourt Brace.

12. Gaffney, Timothy R. 1996. *Grandpa Takes Me to the Moon.* New York: Tambourine Books.

13. George, William T. 1991. *Fishing at Long Pond.* New York: Greenwillow Books.

14. Griffith, Helen, V. 1995. *Grandaddy's Stars.* New York: Greenwillow Books.

15. Hendry, Diana. 1999. *The Very Noisy Night.* New York: Dutton Children's Books.

16. Hines, Anna Grossnickle. 1993. *Gramma's Walk.* New York: Greenwillow Books.

17. Holman, Sandy Lynne. 1995. *Grandpa, Is Everything Black Bad?* Davis, CA: Culture Coop.

18. Jessup, Harley. 1999. *Grandma Summer.* New York: Viking.

19. Johnston, Tony. 1991. *Grandpa's Song.* New York: Dial Books for Young Readers.

20. Lyon, George Ella. 1990. *Basket.* New York: Orchard Books.

21. Oppenheim, Shulamith Levey. 1994. *Fireflies for Nathan.* New York: Tambourine Books.

22. Polacco, Patricia. 1996. *The Trees of the Dancing Goats.* New York: Simon & Schuster Books for Young Readers.

23. Rice, Eve. 1990. *At Grammy's House.* New York: Greenwillow Books.

24. Rogers, Paul. 1994. *A Letter to Grandma.* New York: Atheneum.

25. Russo, Marisabina. 1996. *Grandpa Abe.* New York: Greenwillow Books.

26. Sathre, Vivian. 1997. *On Grandpa's Farm.* Boston: Houghton Mifflin.

27. Scheller, Melanie. 1992. *My Grandfather's Hat.* New York: McElderry Books.

28. Scott, Ann Herbert. 1990. *Grandmother's Chair.* New York: Clarion Books.

29. Silverman, Erica. 1990. *On Grandma's Roof.* New York: Macmillan.

30. Smith, Maggie. 1992. *My Grandma's Chair.* New York: Lothrop, Lee & Shepard Books.

31. Tompert, Ann. 1990. *Grandfather Tang's Story.* New York: Crown.

32. Wayland, April Halprin. 1995. *It's Not My Turn To Look For Grandma!* New York: Knopf.

33. Wild, Margaret. 1994. *Our Granny.* New York: Ticknor & Fields.

34. Wilder, Laura Ingalls. 1994. *Dance at Grandpa's.* New York: HarperCollins.

35. Zalben, Jane Breskin. 1997. *Pearl's Marigolds for Grandpa.* New York: Simon & Schuster Books for Young Readers.

BOOKS SENIORS ENJOY

1. Brokaw, Tom. 2001. *An Album of Memories.* New York: Random House.

2. Canfield, Jack, et al. 2000. *Chicken Soup for the Golden Soul: Heartwarming Stories for People 60 and Over.* Deerfield Beach, FL: Health Communications.

3. Carter, Jimmy. 1998. *The Virtues of Aging.* New York: Ballantine.

4. Dawson, George. 2000. *Life Is So Good.* New York: Random House.

5. Delaney, Sarah. 1997. *On My Own at 107.* San Francisco: HarperSanFrancisco.

6. Delany, Sarah. 1993. *Having Our Say: The Delany Sisters' First 100 Years.* New York: Kodansha International.

7. Dychtwald, Ken. 1999. *Age Power: How the 21st Century Will be Ruled by the New Old.* New York: J.P. Tarcher/Putnam.

8. Ellis, Albert and Emmett Velton. 1998. *Optimal Aging (Get Over Getting Older).* Chicago: Open Court.

9. Foveaux, Jessie. 1997. *Any Given Day: The Life and Times of Jesse Brown Foveaux.* New York: Warner Books.

10. Gottfried, Martin. 1996. *George Burns and The Hundred-Year Dash.* New York: Simon & Schuster.

11. Haddock, Doris. 2001. *Granny D: Walking Across American in My 90th Year.* New York: Villard Books.

12. Hird, Thora. 1998. *Thora Hird's Book of Bygones.* Oxford, England: Isis Large Print.

13. Kalian, Bob and Linda. 1999. *The Best Free Things for Seniors.* New York: Roblin Press.

14. Komaiko, Leah. 1999. *Am I Old Yet?* New York: St. Martin's Press.

15. Linkletter, Art. 1988. *Old Age is Not for Sissies: Choices for Senior Americans.* New York: Viking.

16. Mosier, Leslie. 1990. *Older and Growing.* Waco, TX: Multi-Media Productions.

17. Pogrebin, Letty Cottin. 1996. *Getting Over Getting Older.* Boston: Little, Brown.

18. Strnad, Ed. 1997. *Getting Old Sucks: But It Sure Beats the Alternative.* CCC Productions.

19. Weaver, Francis. 1996. *The Girls with the Grandmother Faces.* New York: Hyperion.

MORE PROGRAM RESOURCES

1. Ammon, Bette D., and Gale W. Sherman. 1996. *Worth a Thousand Words: an Annotated Guide to Picture Books for Older Readers.* Englewood, CO: Libraries Unlimited.

2. Chrisman, Dorothy. 1993. *Body Recall. A Program of Physical Fitness for the Adult.* Richmond, KY: Copyrite Printing.

3. Cordrey, Cindy, CMT-BC. 1994. *Hidden Treasures. Music and Memory Activities for People With Alzheimers.* Mt. Airy, MD: Eldersong.

4. *Elder-Berries Library Programs for Older Adults.* 1998. Columbus, OH: Ohio Library Council.

5. Mason Crest (www.masoncrest.com) has published a twenty-one volume set about North American folklore that is perfect for creating programs exploring our cultural traditions. A sampling of available titles include:

   Bonnice, Sherry. *Christmas and Santa Claus Folklore.*

   Libal, Autumn. *Folk Proverbs and Riddles.*

   Libal, Joyce. *Folk Games.*

   Sanna, Ellyn. *Food Folklore.*

   Sieling, Peter. *Folk Medicine.*

6. Mates, Barbara T. 2003. *5-Star Programming and Services for Your 55+ Library Customers.* Chicago: American Library Association.

7. National Institute on Aging. 2001. *Resource Directory for Older People.* Bethesda, MD: Office of Communications and Public Liaison.

8. "Senior's Dance and Exercise Videos." www.centralhome.com/ballroomcountry/senior_citizen_dance_and_exercis.htm.

9. Missouri State Library, Library Development. "Serving Seniors: A Resource Manual for Missouri Libraries." www.sos.state.mo.us/library/development/services/seniors/manual/default.asp.

APPENDIX F: ESL AND INTERNATIONAL RESOURCES

OVERVIEW

Many libraries are already serving multicultural communities, but as the immigrant population grows, more resources are needed to help more libraries meet the demands of their diverse patronage. This is a list of resources recommended by librarians on our questionnaires and on the electronic discussion lists.

1. AARP. "International Affairs." www.aarp.org/inter national/Articles/a2002-08-07-networks.

2. Queens Borough Public Library "International Resource Center." www.queenslibrary.org/ irc/index .asp.

3. Administration on Aging. "Serving Our Hispanic American Elders." www.aoa.gov/press/fact/alpha/ fact_serving_hispanicamer.asp.

4. "The Learning Light." www.thelearninglight.org. (This site has helpful material for libraries serving Spanish speaking patrons. There are free library phrase lists and a Dewey Classification list in Spanish in pdf format.)

5. Thorndike Large Print in Spanish. www.gale group.com/thorndike.

6. American Library Association. "Guidelines for Library Services to Hispanics." www.ala.org/ Content/NavigationMenu/RUSA/Professional_Tool s4/Reference_Guidelines/Guidelines_for_Library_ Services_to_Hispanics.htm.

7. University of Illinois Urbana-Champaign. "A Librarian's Guide to Latino Services." http://leep.lis. uiuc.edu/seworkspace/LatinoService/collecte.htm.

INDEX

ABOUT THE AUTHORS

RoseMary Honnold is the Young Adult Services Coordinator at Coshocton Public Library in Coshocton, Ohio. She is the creator of the *See YA Around* Web site at www.cplrmh.com and the author of *101+ Teen Programs That Work*. She is a member of the MOLO Regional Library System Young Adult Special Interest Group, serves on the Ohio Library Council Young Adult Division Action Council, and is a member of the Young Adult Library Services Association and the American Library Association. RoseMary has presented several conference sessions and workshops on programming. *Serving Seniors: a How-To-Do-It Manual for Librarians* is her second book.

Saralyn A. Mesaros is the Senior Services Coordinator at Coshocton Public Library. Saralyn is a member of the MOLO Regional Library System Outreach Special Interest Group and Ohio Library Council. Saralyn has shared senior program ideas at MOLO and OLC presentations. *Serving Seniors: a How-To-Do-It Manual for Librarians* is Saralyn's first book.